Closing
the
Engagement
Gap

Closing the Engagement Gap

How Great Companies Unlock Employee Potential for Superior Results

Julie Gebauer and Don Lowman

OF TOWERS PERRIN

with Joanne Gordon

PORTFOLIO

PORTFOLIO

Published by the Penguin Group

Penguin Group (USA) Inc., 375 Hudson Street, New York, New York 10014, U.S.A.
Penguin Group (Canada), 90 Eglinton Avenue East, Suite 700, Toronto, Ontario,
Canada M4P 2Y3 (a division of Pearson Penguin Canada Inc.)
Penguin Books Ltd, 80 Strand, London WC2R 0RL, England
Penguin Ireland, 25 St. Stephen's Green, Dublin 2, Ireland (a division of Penguin Books Ltd)
Penguin Books Australia Ltd, 250 Camberwell Road, Camberwell, Victoria 3124, Australia
(a division of Pearson Australia Group Pty Ltd)
Penguin Books India Pvt Ltd, 11 Community Centre, Panchsheel Park, New Delhi – 110 017, India
Penguin Group (NZ), 67 Apollo Drive, Rosedale, North Shore 0632, New Zealand
(a division of Pearson New Zealand Ltd)
Penguin Books (South Africa) (Pty) Ltd, 24 Sturdee Avenue, Rosebank,
Johannesburg 2196, South Africa

Penguin Books Ltd, Registered Offices: 80 Strand, London WC2R 0RL, England

First published in 2008 by Portfolio, a member of Penguin Group (USA) Inc.

1 3 5 7 9 10 8 6 4 2

Copyright © Towers, Perrin, Forster & Crosby, Inc., 2008
All rights reserved

Charts and graphs courtesy of Towers Perrin

LIBRARY OF CONGRESS CATALOGING-IN-PUBLICATION DATA
Gebauer, Julie.
Closing the engagement gap: how great companies unleash employee potential for superior
results / by Julie Gebauer and Don Lowman, with Joanne Gordon.
p. cm.
Includes index.
ISBN 978-1-59184-238-5
1. Employee motivation.   2. Employee empowerment.   3. Career development.
4. Corporate culture.   5. Organizational commitment.   I. Lowman, Don.   II. Gordon, Joanne.
III. Title.   IV. Subtitle: How great companies unleash employee potential for superior results.
HF5549.5.M63G43 2009
658.3'14—dc22   2008029547

Printed in the United States of America
Designed by Chris Welch

CONTENTS

PREFACE

The most valuable source of high performance and competitive advantage is a workforce that consistently performs at its best. But employees do their best only if they're *engaged* in their work. For more than twenty years we've researched what it means to be engaged, and helped companies around the world understand what it takes to unlock people's potential for improved business results. We wrote *Closing the Engagement Gap* because now, perhaps more than ever, individual employees' attitudes and actions are unavoidably linked to how well organizations perform.

At engagement's core is the notion that most employees want to make a difference. They want to contribute to their worlds—whether on the plant floor or a corporate campus, or in a call center, research facility, or retail outlet. All people bring to the workplace a portfolio of skills, knowledge, experiences, and other attributes such as creativity, agility, discipline, passion, and motivation that they can choose to use on the job, or withhold. Enlightened leaders understand that it's up to them to ensure that employees *choose* to put all of themselves into their work. Enlightened leaders know that people who give 110 percent on the job—who routinely go above and beyond expectations—are engaged in their work. And these leaders also know that engagement is a business imperative, especially in today's complex, global, rapidly changing business environment.

Our perspective on engagement—on what drives people to excel—is informed and shaped by our expertise as well as by our personal histories. Our passion for this topic is rooted in who we are as people, not just what we do professionally.

Julie Gebauer currently leads Towers Perrin's Workforce Effectiveness Practice and is Managing Director of Towers Perrin's organization research business. Over the course of her career, she has held other key management positions and helped some of the largest organizations in the world resolve complex workforce, human resource management, and rewards issues. Julie has spearheaded a number of research efforts, most recently Towers Perrin's *Global Workforce Study*, and has taught executive seminars for several renowned educational institutions, including Harvard University. Julie is also a Fellow of the Society of Actuaries, which means that she is not only a data junkie, but has achieved the highest standing in the field of actuarial science, a profession that values mathematic and statistical analysis of the highest level. Thus, Julie brings a rare level of rigor to the engagement discussion.

But Julie's background plays an even more significant role in shaping her passion about this issue. She grew up in a small Nebraska town, the daughter of a hardworking salesman and a mother who raised seven children while working a multitude of jobs outside the home. "Both my parents influenced my career aspirations and decisions. As our family struggled financially, my mother found ways to make treasures out of things other people tossed away and to create tasty meals from morsels. While she put her heart and soul into building a strong family, she also put significant effort into her work outside the home, whether it was volunteer work or a paying job. I saw times when she was engaged in her work—for example, when the church choir published a song she wrote, or when a supervisor recognized her for her hard work. I also saw times when she was disenchanted—like when the person in charge wouldn't listen to her ideas for raising more money at an event, or for how to make the workplace safer. In all, my mother's experience showed me that hard work is rewarding and engaging when the work environment is right.

"My father showed me how truly enjoyable work could be if I did something I really loved and believed in. He couldn't have been happier working directly with people, building personal relationships, and providing great customer service. These experiences had a profound effect on my career choices and a lasting impact on my leadership style. My parents showed me what it took for them to be engaged, and I've made sure my job incorporated these things: opportunities to provide input, do challenging work, and continue to learn. I also try to pattern what I do as a leader to reflect some key lessons from my parents' experiences: I know it's important to listen closely to what people have to say and to involve others to get better answers, and give people room to grow."

Don Lowman is a Managing Director of Towers Perrin and a member of the firm's Executive Council and Board of Directors. In his twenty-six years with Towers Perrin, he has led several of the firm's lines of business and managed its geographic operations, while also consulting to some of the world's largest and most well-known global companies. Selected by his industry peers as one of the world's Top 25 Consultants in 2003, Don is an expert in the areas of executive compensation, employee rewards, performance metrics, and performance management. Don is an adviser to the boards of directors and senior management of several Fortune 100 companies, and has worked with more than two hundred clients during his career. He speaks frequently on the subjects of executive compensation and leadership performance, and is often sought out for his expert views by those in the media and recently by the U.S. Congress. His behind-the-scenes exposure to what drives leaders to succeed—and fail—is unparalleled.

While Don's perspective has been enriched by working with gifted leaders—and learning from their successes as well as their failures—his most important teacher was much closer to home. "It was my late father who had the greatest influence in shaping my philosophy toward leadership and showing me the important connection that leaders can have with people every day.

"My dad, born into a family of modest means, learned life's hardest lessons when his own father passed away at the age of forty-one. A member of the Greatest Generation, my dad enlisted in the Air Force during World War II at age nineteen, and, after the war, worked his way up from the mailroom to the executive ranks at Standard Oil (now Exxon). He passed away in 2003 at age eighty-three, and in his final days, my dad reflected at length on his life, his experiences, and his most enduring memories. The most important thing, he told me, is not what we do at work, or the accolades we collect for our accomplishments. Rather, it's the quality of the relationships we develop with others, and how the people in our lives remember us, and what we brought to their lives. When he passed away, letters poured in from the surviving members of his squadron in the war, and from dozens of friends and former business acquaintances. Those heartfelt letters cited very personal reflections of the influence my dad had on so many people from different walks of life; and they revealed to me just how much my father had touched others' lives, personally as well as professionally.

"The secret to my father's ability to engage people was in his power to listen and understand what was truly important in others' lives. He showed a sincere personal interest in all he touched, and he related to people in a very genuine way that touched them and let them know they were special and valued. This, I've come to learn firsthand, is one of the shared qualities of many of the world's most engaging leaders."

In many ways, *Closing the Engagement Gap* is an opportunity for us to share our parents' legacies, while simultaneously helping you, our readers, to establish your own legacies at home and at work. You and your organizations have far more power than you realize to drive employee engagement and increase the discretionary effort employees choose to expend in their jobs. You can turn a hidden reservoir of energy, passion, and determination into competitive advantage and superior performance.

While engagement is a personal experience, it's not only accomplished one employee at a time. Some of the actions you can take will engage many people simultaneously. Some of the things you do will be contagious, extending the reach of your engaging efforts well beyond one individual. Our hope is that *Closing the Engagement Gap* allows you to make a more significant imprint on employees, and on your organization, than you previously envisioned.

—Julie Gebauer

—Don Lowman

Closing
the
Engagement
Gap

Closing the
Engagement Gap

We're all searching for an edge. Each of us needs to find an opportunity to help our companies outperform the competition and generate better growth and better margins. Most likely you've undertaken financial reengineering. You've restructured, pursued M&A synergies, and implemented new technologies. But your stakeholders expect more.

A rich source for higher performance is within your reach. It resides within almost every person who works for your organization. Your employees' decisions, attitudes, and actions make—or break—your organization's ability to innovate, deliver superior customer service, and manage costs efficiently. They hold the key to revenue growth and margin improvement.

Unfortunately, this source of performance is not being tapped to its full extent at most companies. But it can be. It must be. To successfully unlock employees' full potential, you and your organization must do one thing right: *engage your people*.

Employee engagement is a term that has come to describe the

deep and broad connection that employees have with a company, as well as their voluntary and enthusiastic commitment to its success. Engaged employees give 110 percent (or more) on behalf of their company, their team, or their division. Full engagement exists when every employee works at the top of his or her game, going the productive extra mile without thinking twice. They ask, "What's in it for *us*?" not just "What's in it for *me*?" Imagine:

- An account manager who picks up his ringing phone at 4:58 p.m. on a Friday rather than letting the call pass to voice mail, even if it means he must stay at work an extra half hour to help a customer.
- An administrative assistant who takes the time to reread a report before it's sent to one of her firm's largest clients and notices inconsistencies that, when pointed out, cause her boss to change the company's underlying recommendations.
- An engineer who comes up with an innovative product idea while attending his son's baseball game and rearranges schedules so his team can begin researching its potential the next day.
- A hospital orderly who works in a bilingual community and voluntarily enrolls in company-provided Spanish classes so he can better communicate with patients—even if it is just to ask how they're feeling—as he transfers them from one room to another.
- A waiter who treats his customers as special guests and creates a memorable dining experience by sharing insights about each item on the menu and what makes it unique.
- A cost-conscious employee who takes small steps to save money, such as taking public transportation to meetings rather than pricier taxis and limos, or using old company letterhead

to print out internal documents rather than throwing out reams of perfectly good paper.

- An office manager who spends free time collecting overdue invoices—a task not part of her regular duties—because she understands what the revenue means for the success of her branch.

Examples like these show up every day as engaged employees make critical contributions to organizational performance. However, there are countless missed opportunities. And it's easy to envision the impact of converting those opportunities—multiplied across thousands of workers every day—on customer service, costs, revenue, and shareholder value.

Engaged employees not only help companies succeed in times of growth, but also help their companies weather an economic downturn or other challenging events that could adversely affect results. People's energy, dedication, and desire to contribute not only help generate and sustain results in good times, but bring resiliency and optimism to the workplace in tough times, shortening the period needed to turn a business around.

No organization should risk leaving employee engagement to chance, hoping it will just happen. Its benefits, which are undeniable, are too important: consistent brand delivery, creativity, exceptional customer service and support, innovation, and day-to-day commitment to product and process excellence. We have a large body of compelling evidence, which we share throughout this book, proving that highly engaged workers deliver better business performance. In turn, better business results improve employee engagement. It's a virtuous, prosperous circle.

Engagement is much more than an intellectually appealing topic. It's a bottom-line issue. Most companies have an opportunity to realize significant performance improvements with little new financial investment. But doing so requires that they—that you—understand the leadership and management behaviors and specific organizational processes and systems that are necessary to engage employees, and to capture their full potential and sustained commitment. We intend to help everyone who runs a business, sets policy, leads a workforce, manages a project, or supervises others to grasp the notion of engagement—from the theoretical to the practical—so they can do their part to improve business outcomes regardless of where they sit in the organization. Our intent is straightforward: we want to help you and the people throughout your organization become more engaging leaders, and more engaged workers.

We hope this book will enlighten you and inspire you to realize your own potential as a leader. We believe it will give you the tools to help others recognize their own potential as professionals. That potential is waiting to be tapped.

The Engagement Gap: An Untapped Opportunity for Higher Performance

Tragically, most organizations have yet to harness the full power of employee engagement, failing to achieve the significant performance lift that a fully engaged workforce can deliver. Our research is unequivocal on this point. While the vast majority of people we survey regularly say they want to give more to their companies, only a fifth of the global workforce in our most recent study is currently fully engaged. Put another way:

> Four out of every five workers worldwide are not delivering their full potential to help their organizations succeed.

Many of the world's workers (41 percent) are what we call "enrolled," meaning they are capable, they care, and they're ready to be engaged. Unfortunately, they are not being inspired or motivated—by their organizations or their bosses—to consistently put forth discretionary effort. As for the rest of the global employee population, they are either disenchanted (30 percent) or disengaged (8 percent). While the disenchanted report some connection with their companies that could be converted to stronger engagement, the disengaged group show virtually no positive connections with their organizations. While the disengaged may not be destroying value, they aren't performing anywhere near their true capability, and have no intention of doing so.

Think about your own colleagues, teams, and departments. How many people routinely go the extra mile? Are they learning new skills and growing their careers? How inspired are your colleagues when it comes to helping your organization meet its goals? How well do employees understand the role they play in the company's success? And do people feel adequately appreciated and rewarded for the efforts they put forth? Do employees truly believe your organization and its leaders have a sincere interest in their well-being?

Now, turn the tables, and ask yourself these questions. As a leader and a direct manager of others, do you motivate people to go the extra mile? Do you help people in the organization develop new skills and advance their careers? Do you inspire employees to do what it takes so the organization can meet its strategic goals? Do you inform people about how they contribute to the organization's performance? Do you show appreciation and recognize the efforts of work well done? Do you sincerely care about the people who work for the company, and for you, and let them know it?

If you can't respond affirmatively to most of these questions, there is probably a discrepancy between the effort your people are actually putting forth and what they are capable of giving. This discrepancy is what we call "the engagement gap." In a nutshell, the engagement gap is the difference between the discretionary effort that employees are willing to give their employers and employers' ability to garner that effort from a significant portion of their workforce.

The tools we provide in this book will help you close that gap.

The Engagement-Performance Link:
A Virtuous Circle

"There are only three measurements that tell you nearly everything you need to know about your organization's overall performance: employee engagement, customer satisfaction, and cash flow," wrote former GE Chairman and CEO Jack Welch in *BusinessWeek* in May 2006. He went on: "It goes without saying that no company, small or large, can win over the long run without energized employees who believe in the mission and understand how to achieve it . . ."

We agree. Our own perspectives about engagement are informed by three primary sources of information.

The first is our firm's long-standing body of research into the attitudes of employees around the world, and the workplace elements that drive attraction, retention, and engagement. Towers Perrin's most recent study, the *2007–2008 Global Workforce Study,* titled *Closing the Engagement Gap: A Roadmap for Driving Superior Business Performance,* is the primary source for most of the engagement data in this book. (See Exhibit A for an overview of the *Global Workforce Study.*) This study offers the most complete view of workforce attitudes available today, establishing an undeniable link between employee engagement and business performance, and providing a clear picture of the workplace attributes that drive engagement.

Our perspective on engagement is also based on our combined experience working closely with senior business leaders in a wide range of organizations across geographies and industries.

Exhibit A: Towers Perrin *Global Workforce Study*

Towers Perrin's *2007-2008 Global Workforce Study* draws on two unique sources of data that come directly from employees. The first is an online polling survey administered to a randomly chosen group of close to 90,000 employees working full-time for midsize to large organizations in eighteen countries worldwide, including the United States, China, Canada, France, the United Kingdom, and India. A profile of this group, which represents every age category, key job type, and experience level, appears below.

The second source is the world's largest employee normative database, with data that is updated annually from more than 2 million employees at a range of companies in more than forty countries, including those with above- and below-average financial performance.

Global Workforce Survey Respondents ... at a Glance

GENDER		AGE		YEARS AT COMPANY		COMPANY SIZE	
Male	65%	18-24	11%	< 1 year	11%	250-999	29%
Female	35%	25-34	33%	1-4 years	34%	1,000-2,499	.19%
		35-44	28%	5-9 years	23%	2,500-4,999	10%
		45-54	20%	10-14 years	11%	5,000-14,999	15%
		55 +	8%	15+ years	21%	15,000+	27%

RESPONDENTS BY COUNTRY

Belgium	1,000	India	4,500	Poland	1,000
Brazil	1,500	Italy	1,000	Russia	1,000
Canada	5,000	Japan	4,000	Spain	1,000
China	6,000	Korea	1,000	Switzerland	1,000
France	5,000	Mexico	1,000	United Kingdom	5,000
Germany	3,000	Netherlands	2,500	United States	41,500

The final source comes from real life. For more than a year, we sought out and interviewed people in top-performing organizations, candidly asking their senior leaders, policy makers, HR experts, and managers at every level how they engage their workforce and their direct reports. Perhaps most telling, we asked employees themselves how and why they go above and beyond to deliver results that exceed expectations and contribute to the organization's growth. Their stories bring our data to life, providing a profound, often surprising degree of insight into what makes workers tick, and how managers can tap those drivers.

While some people may believe the connection between employee engagement and business performance is obvious, it's still not well understood by most. Some hard-edged business leaders believe it's a waste of time to think about so-called soft stuff. Skeptics say the engagement-performance link is too good to be true—or too tough to measure—so they ignore it. And others are convinced that nothing they do will change the way employees feel or act.

They're all missing a valuable truth. *Engagement is not soft, and its impact can be measured and is measured and acted upon by many successful organizations.*

Three of our firm's recent studies dramatically illustrate this point. In one, we looked at fifty global companies over a year, correlating their employee engagement levels with their financial results. The companies with high employee engagement had a 19 percent increase in operating income and almost a 28 percent growth in earnings per share. Conversely, companies with low levels of engagement saw operating income drop more than 32 percent and earnings per share decline 11 percent.

In a similar study over a longer time horizon—involving forty global companies over three years—we found a spread of more than 5 percentage points in operating margin and more than 3 percentage points in net profit margin between the companies with high employee engagement and those with low engagement.

The third study draws on companies in our High Performance Engagement Index. This group of companies, with higher levels of engagement, generated annual shareholder returns that were 9.3 percentage points higher than the return for the S&P 500 index for the period 2002–2006.

A large body of research outside our own confirms the strong correlation between employee engagement and company performance. Yet, none of the studies definitively answers the question "Which comes first, performance or engagement?" The fact of the matter is that it's hard to say and, we believe, beside the point. What matters most is that engagement and performance feed each other in a continuous virtuous circle. It's not important whether you enter this circle from an engagement perspective or from a performance perspective. What does matter is that you enter the circle at all, and that you stay the course.

Engagement, Defined

Before moving forward, we want to be absolutely clear about the meaning of engagement and what constitutes the state of "being engaged."

As we previously stated, employee engagement is a deep and broad connection that employees have with a company that results in a willingness to go above and beyond what's expected of them to help their company succeed. This connection has to occur at three levels:

- The rational (the head): how well employees understand their roles and responsibilities; the "thinking" part of the equation.
- The emotional (the heart): how much passion and energy they bring to their work; the "feeling" part of the equation.

- The motivational (the hands): how well they perform in their roles; the "acting" part of the equation.

Put another way, an engaged employee *understands* what to do to help her company succeed, she *feels* emotionally connected to the organization and its leaders, and she is willing to put that knowledge and emotion into *action* to improve performance, her own and the organization's.

One or two of these connections is not enough to create true engagement. Someone who understands what to do for the company, but doesn't have an emotional tie to it, might be just as happy doing his job at the competitor down the street. Another person who is passionate about the company and its brands, but doesn't understand how her job enables the company to achieve its goals, might make poor choices about how to spend her time on the job.

It's important to clarify that engagement is not synonymous with company loyalty, which is simply a willingness or commitment to stay with the company. Neither is engagement equivalent to occupational dedication, or the degree to which people identify with their chosen careers or professional craft. People committed to their occupation likely work hard and enthusiastically, but have little or no loyalty to their employer, and may be quick to jump from one company to another. Finally, engagement is not the same as happiness. That's not to say that a company shouldn't be pleased if its workers describe themselves as happy. But, happy workers are not necessarily productive; indeed, it's possible for an employee to love a job or a company without contributing much.

Unlike these other attributes, engagement is a meaningful and relevant business metric because, as we've seen, it correlates so highly to business performance.

The Top Ten Global Engagement Drivers

In the summer of 2007, we went to Las Vegas to meet the president and employees of MGM Grand, one of the premier hotels in the portfolio of MGM Mirage, the world's largest hotel and casino operator. Under the leadership of its COO and president, Gamal Aziz (whom we'll meet in chapter 6), MGM Grand has transformed itself from a good hotel and casino into a world-class entertainment destination that houses top-rated restaurants, hosts sold-out concerts and top-rated sporting events, produces original shows, and scores among the highest rankings for service and hospitality. We were in Las Vegas to see firsthand how MGM Grand's almost 10,000 employees pull it off.

When we arrived at the airport, a middle-aged gentleman from the hotel, impeccably dressed in a three-piece suit, greeted us, took our luggage, and escorted us to a silver Maybach, one of several in a fleet that routinely take guests to and from the hotel. We chatted amicably with the driver during our brief ride. He was personable without being intrusive or insincere, and his overall demeanor made us feel at home and like VIPs. More than a driver, he was a gracious host. Compare this to the all-too-familiar alternative: a sullen or disgruntled driver who talks on his cell phone during the drive, maintains a dirty car interior, or has no idea how to get to the destination. Our MGM Grand driver's hospitable attitude and presence helped kick-start a memorable experience for us that, as we shall see, is intrinsic to MGM Grand's competitive strategy.

As we pulled up to the hotel's entrance, we asked the driver how long he had worked for MGM Grand.

"Nine years," he said.

We asked why he had stayed at the company for so long when there were so many other places in Vegas to work.

"Great insurance," he answered. "They are great at solving problems that come up, and they have an open-door policy." This was not a terribly surprising answer. Our research had told us that health care and other benefits are a key reason people choose to work for and stay at a company in the United States. However, benefits do not affect the level of effort people put forth on the job. Our own intuition told us that something more than health insurance—and more than a potential tip—motivated our driver's extremely hospitable behavior on that hot summer afternoon.

If we had asked why he liked his job and obviously put so much energy into it—not why he stayed—we would have gotten a very different answer, as we did with his colleague who drove us back to the airport after our two-day visit. This second gentleman was also impeccably dressed and friendly without being intrusive, asking about our visit and making us feel as if a familiar friend, not a hired hand, was escorting us on our journey home. As we approached the airport's departure terminal, we asked this driver if he enjoyed working for MGM Grand.

He grinned. "Absolutely!" We asked why, and this time we heard about more than medical coverage. "Mr. Aziz," he said, referring to MGM Grand's president. "Of course, I've met him, and I've never seen such a big executive pay such attention to small details. He even picked out the color of these cars!"

Note that we later asked MGM Grand if it told the drivers we were writing a book about the company and its employees, information that might have affected how they treated us. Corrine Clement, an executive director at MGM Grand and our primary contact, told us: "Grounding the limo drivers was not something I did, but it's a good idea for us with future guests!"

With that potential bias out of the way, our driver anecdotes illustrate three points.

First, what drives employees to stay at a company is not necessarily the same thing that drives them to excel on the job. Second, senior leaders are perhaps the most potent force—even more powerful than one's direct boss—when it comes to engaging workers. And third, every engaged employee makes a difference. While a single limo driver is hardly responsible for increasing MGM Grand's revenues and earnings on his own, one employee's positive attitude and value-added behavior manifested in thousands of other employees inevitably improves overall performance.

Our *Global Workforce Study* helped us more fully understand what factors engage employees, as well as the role that companies can play in engaging their workforce. We identified the top ten items that drive employee engagement around the world. They are listed below in descending order of impact:

1. Senior management's sincere interest in employee well-being.
2. The opportunity an employee has to improve skills and capabilities.
3. The organization's reputation for social responsibility.
4. The opportunity an employee has to provide input into decision making in his department.
5. The organization's ability to quickly resolve customer concerns.
6. An individual employee's own readiness to set high personal standards.
7. Excellent career advancement opportunities.
8. An individual employee's interest in challenging work assignments.
9. An individual's relationship with her supervisor.
10. The organization's encouragement of innovative thinking.

These top ten global drivers are the key to unlocking employee engagement and improving business performance. They do, of course, vary by country (see Exhibit B for some illustrative distinctions across geography) as well as by various demographic factors, such as age. While these are universal attributes that make a difference in eliciting engagement in almost every workplace, their relative influence does shift across cultures and generations, among other factors.

Exhibit B: Top Engagement Drivers in Representative Countries

Brazil

1. Organization rewards outstanding customer service.
2. Improved my skills and capabilities over last year.
3. Senior management sincerely interested in employee well-being.
4. Enjoy challenging work assignments that broaden skills.
5. Organization invests in innovative products/services.

China

1. Have excellent career advancement opportunities.
2. Organization encourages innovative thinking.
3. Organization's reputation for financial stability.
4. Good collaboration across units.
5. Senior management sincerely interested in employee well-being.

Germany

1. Senior management sincerely interested in employee well-being.
2. Appropriate amount of decision-making authority to do job well.
3. Organization's reputation for social responsibility.
4. Seek opportunities to develop new skills.
5. Manager inspires enthusiasm for work.

Top Engagement Drivers in Representative Countries
(continued)

India

1. Input into decision making in my department.
2. Senior management's actions consistent with company values.
3. Organization's reputation for social responsibility.
4. Seek opportunities to develop new skills.
5. Have excellent career advancement opportunities.

United Kingdom

1. Senior management sincerely interested in employee well-being.
2. Improved my skills and capabilities over last year.
3. Organization quickly resolves customer concerns.
4. Appropriate amount of decision-making authority to do job well.
5. Organization's reputation for social responsibility.

United States

1. Senior management sincerely interested in employee well-being.
2. Improved my skills and capabilities over last year.
3. Organization's reputation for social responsibility.
4. Input into decision making in my department.
5. Organization quickly resolves customer concerns.

At the same time, there is remarkable consistency among the drivers. The number one driver—*senior management's sincere interest in employee well-being*—is the top engagement driver not only globally, but also in seven of the eighteen countries in our study. It's also on the top ten lists in all but six countries. This finding speaks to the enormous influence that a company's top leaders have on every member of the workforce, from a vice president to, in the case of MGM Grand, a driver.

It may be tempting for many leaders and managers to dismiss the engagement drivers as mere common sense. It may also be tempting to rationalize that workers around the world have negative perceptions about how well their companies are delivering on the engagement drivers because they have unrealistically high expectations. But don't get caught in these traps. If the attributes were so obvious and so easy for organizations to weave into their cultures, we'd see far higher levels of engagement and more positive responses from employees.

As the data below show, our global survey respondents—almost 90,000 employees—believe their organizations have room for improvement in delivering on many of engagement's key drivers. Specifically:

- Only 38 percent of employees believe that their senior management is sincerely interested in their well-being.
- 65 percent say they had the opportunity to improve their skills and capabilities over the past year.
- 57 percent believe their organization has a good reputation for social responsibility.
- 67 percent say they have input into decision-making.
- 61 percent say their organization quickly resolves customer concerns.
- 63 percent say they set high personal standards.
- 36 percent believe they have excellent career advancement opportunities.
- 50 percent say their organization encourages innovative thinking.

The good news is that these statistics point the way toward positive change because they represent a significant and encouraging opportunity to make workplace investments that make a real difference to people.

What, then, can organizations, their leaders, and managers at every level do to close the engagement gap?

Five Actions to Convert the Enrolled and Enlist the Disenchanted

Recall that 41 percent of global workers are enrolled, but not yet engaged, and 30 percent are disenchanted. Moving these workers up the engagement spectrum is the key to increasing performance.

Building on the drivers of engagement that we derive through statistical analysis, and related personal reflections from employees themselves, we isolated five interrelated courses of action that will increase engagement and, ultimately, performance and competitive advantage. These action areas form the basis of *Closing the Engagement Gap* and are the focus of the ensuing chapters.

Know Them

Grow Them

Inspire Them

Involve Them

Reward Them

When organizations and leaders at every level Know, Grow, Inspire, Involve, and Reward employees in the right ways, these workers will be much more likely to give more value-adding discretionary effort. That extra effort is the difference between good customer service and great customer service. It's the difference between meeting sales quotas and exceeding them, between tolerating problems and solving them, and between wasting thousands of dollars and saving millions. In short, engagement is the difference between ordinary and extraordinary performance.

Each of our action areas includes an array of behaviors, policies, and programs that are ultimately in the hands of everyone in the workforce—from C-level executives to human resources professionals, from first-line managers to individual employees. When everyone in an organization understands and gets behind these actions—executing in ways most appropriate for their level and role—they collectively snowball into extraordinary performance for the team, unit, division, and organization itself.

We'll speak to these four groups—CEOs, HR leaders, managers, and all other employees—throughout the book and conclude with a tactical look at how each group can ramp up engagement across these action areas within its own unique sphere and set of responsibilities. For now, here's an overview of the five areas.

Know Them

Organizations need to put their workforce under the same microscope that they apply to their customers. Just as consumers choose which products to buy, employees make choices every day about which organization to work for, what tasks they will undertake, and how much to focus once on the job. Taking time to know what's important to each individual employee, as well as to your workforce as a whole, is the first step toward securing discretionary effort and changing the way employees view their work.

Grow Them

Professional growth and intellectual challenge are priorities for most people, both inside and outside the workplace. People across industries want short- and long-term opportunities to improve their skills and capabilities. To effectively grow employees as well as the organization, senior leaders must foster a culture of ongoing learning and education. We will show you how to create a learning culture that ensures employees have the right skills and knowledge to further the business objectives that drive financial growth, while simultaneously furthering their own careers.

INSPIRE THEM

Most people want to have an emotional connection to their work as well as to the organizations for which they work. True, few employees actually describe what they're looking for as an "emotional connection." But consider the following to illustrate what we mean. Employees are more inclined to give discretionary effort when purpose and meaning infuse their day-to-day activities and long-term agendas. And, when employees respect their managers and colleagues, they are more inspired to meet and exceed expectations. Inspiration comes about in large part by what leaders and managers emphasize and prioritize, and how clearly and effectively they communicate those priorities. We discuss how engaging leaders, to effectively inspire, create a sense of pride in the work they and the company do, and show a sincere interest in employees' well-being.

INVOLVE THEM

People give discretionary effort when they feel they are active participants in their employers' missions, not passive players just following orders. This means people must be knowledgeable about the business for which they work, be treated as valued contributors, and have the freedom to act in ways that they believe will enhance overall performance. Effectively involving employees requires senior leaders and direct managers to do four things, which we explain in detail: inform employees about business operations and external challenges; gather employee input; create collaborative opportunities with colleagues; and give people freedom to act in ways that improve operations, reduce costs, and assist customers.

Reward Them

Rewards encompass all the things employees receive in exchange for their work. This includes the obvious and immediate forms of monetary compensation, including salary, health care benefits, pension benefits, and other financial benefits. But rewards also include nonfinancial elements, like appreciation and recognition. It's this last type of reward that has the greatest potential to boost engagement. However, pay and benefits can't be overlooked. While they may not induce people to put in extra effort on the job, they can disengage people if they are viewed as unfair or uncompetitive, undermining the effect of other efforts to engage. In our chapter dedicated to rewarding employees, we'll explore what constitutes "right" and offer concrete steps, anecdotes and, perhaps most important, employee perspectives on rewards that mean the most.

Taken together, these five action areas —Know, Grow, Inspire, Involve, and Reward—build the three connections required for engagement: head, heart, and hands. To create a rational connection and tap employees' intellect and understanding, an organization must create a clear link between the employee's job and the company's strategy, and clarify individual career opportunities. To appeal to the heart, leaders and managers must establish a sense of pride, inspire employees to do great work, and improve employee confidence.

To make sure that employees put their hands to work smartly and productively, organizations must clearly demonstrate what behaviors and actions can make the biggest difference to the company and focus employees on the specific actions and tasks that can make that difference. When all of these areas are addressed with consistency, workers willingly and enthusiastically put forth extra time, energy, and brainpower to help their companies compete and succeed.

Nowhere is the rational-emotional-motivational connection more obvious than in the interviews we conducted with workers at engaging organizations. Let's meet the organizations whose programs and employees we refer to throughout the book.

The Engaging Eight

Capturing engagement "in the act" is a difficult task but incredibly worthwhile, especially for anyone who still doubts its power. Workers' real-life experiences and voices add profound credibility and insight to the discussion. Let's be honest. You can disagree with experts and consultants. And you can debate research. But it's tough to argue with individuals—a plant supervisor in Michigan, a middle manager in New Jersey, an executive assistant in Philadelphia, a waiter in Las Vegas, a salesperson in California, a vice president in India—who testify that they willingly and gladly give 110 percent effort (and then some), and explain why.

The organizations we chose to profile include some companies that are Towers Perrin clients and some that are not. As a group, we refer to them as the Engaging Eight. While none of the Engaging Eight organizations would claim to have completely solved its engagement challenge, each has an abiding belief that engagement matters a lot.

What follows are brief overviews of the Engaging Eight's respective businesses.

CAMPBELL SOUP COMPANY

The $7.86 billion (2007 net sales) Campbell Soup Company sells soup, food, beverages, and sauces in 120 countries under its name-sake brand as well as twenty others, including Swanson, V8, Pepperidge Farm, Erasco (Germany), Liebig (France), and Arnott's (Asia Pacific). The 137-year-old Camden, New Jersey–based company was foundering in the late 1990s. In 2001, Douglas R. Conant took over as president and CEO in an effort to revive the then-ailing brand. He's done so with an emphasis on product quality, innovation (easy-to-open pop-top cans, for instance, and new supermarket shelving systems), increased marketing, and reinvigorating the workforce.

Conant's goal was to increase total shareholder return and employee engagement. He has succeeded. Compounded over a three-year period (2005, 2006, and 2007), Campbell's total return to shareholders was 8.5 percent, and its operating earnings increased 3 percent. Average return on equity for Campbell during the same three-year period was 54 percent.

Engagement levels have also jumped in the past several years. Campbell employs 19,000 people worldwide, and in 2008 the ratio of actively engaged to actively disengaged employees is 12:1, versus 2:1 in 2003. For its top 350 executives, the engaged-to-disengaged ratio is 35:1, a dramatic improvement from 1:1 in 2001. Campbell has also been named one of the best places to work in the city of Philadelphia, in the states of New Jersey and Connecticut, as well as in Canada overall.

Wall Street analysts and investors have credited CEO Conant with Campbell's turnaround. The veteran food-industry executive remains a staunch champion of engagement. "We have to win in the workplace before we can win in the marketplace," he told us, just as he tells employees and shareholders. "I'm obsessed with keeping engagement front and center and keeping up energy around it."

EMC CORPORATION

The $13 billion Hopkinton, Massachusetts–based technology organization helps companies in virtually every industry store, secure, and optimize their most valuable data. As the self-described "caretaker for more than two-thirds of the world's most essential information," EMC's technologies are the backbone to ubiquitous services such as ATM transactions, mobile phones, stock trades, air travel, and Internet use.

EMC hit a low point in its thirty-year history after the September 11, 2001, terrorist attacks. The recession that followed cut EMC's revenue almost in half, to less than $6 billion. Its subsequent transformation—*BusinessWeek* magazine called it "the most stunning turnaround in the history of technology"—emphasized innovation, quality, and customer service. In 2008, EMC's approximately $33 billion market capitalization put it among the top ten technology organizations in the world. Between 2002 and spring 2008, EMC had acquired more than forty companies, and 100 percent of its current revenue is derived from products introduced in the previous eighteen months.

Compounded over a three-year period (2005, 2006, and 2007), EMC's total return to shareholders was 7.6 percent, and its operating earnings increased 17.5 percent. Average return on equity for EMC during the same three-year period was 11.5 percent.

In 2007, EMC's 37,000 people in fifty countries reported 82 percent job satisfaction, six points higher than the composite of leading organizations against which EMC benchmarks itself. Many of EMC's specific employee measurements reflect engagement's most important tenets: 91 percent say their manager treats them with respect and encourages them to act with integrity and in accordance with EMC policies; 91 percent say they understand how their job fits into the organization's goals and objectives; and 89 percent feel the work they do impacts the customer experience.

In 2006, *Institutional Investor* named CEO Joseph Tucci top CEO in the IT hardware industry for the second year in a row. His motto—"Put EMC first, your people second, and yourself third"—reflects EMC's strategic differentiators of quality and service, and his approach to people management.

HONEYWELL INTERNATIONAL

In 2007, Morristown, New Jersey–based Honeywell derived $34.6 billion in revenues from its diverse portfolio of aerospace products and services, control technologies, automotive products, turbochargers, and specialty materials. Recent years of success have come after fragmentation and frustration, including an enormous merger with Allied-Signal in the late 1990s, and a failed, distracting takeover attempt by GE. Today, CEO Dave Cote's growth strategy focuses on global expansion, product innovation, and operational excellence (efficiency, safety, and cost saving) at Honeywell's offices and plants in more than one hundred countries.

When Cote joined the organization, Honeywell was not performing well. Since he became chief executive in 2002, Honeywell's revenue is up 55 percent. In 2007, cash flow from operations hit $3.9 billion, and between 2002 and 2007, Honeywell had a total return to shareholders of 187 percent. Compounded over a three-year period (2005, 2006, and 2007), Honeywell's operating earnings were up 20 percent. Average return on equity for Honeywell during the same three-year period was 21 percent.

Each quarter, Honeywell surveys employees after CEO Dave Cote holds an electronic town hall meeting, during which he reviews the company's performance and goals. These survey results—which include direct quotes from respondents that are shared with senior management—provide ongoing insight into employees' mind-sets and reflect the major tenets of employee engagement. In January 2008, for example, 83 percent of some 5,000 survey respondents said they had an improved understanding of the company's overall direction and were clear on what they needed to do to contribute.

Cote embraces a pragmatic management philosophy that stems from his own beginnings as an hourly employee in a metal-pressing plant. "People," he says, "are the ultimate differentiator."

McKesson Corporation

Ranked number eighteen among *Fortune*'s largest American corporations and number five on that magazine's list of World's Most Admired Companies, San Francisco–based McKesson is a global provider of wholesale health care products, drugs, and supplies. Its customers include 44 percent of U.S. pharmacies and more than 50 percent of its hospitals. While pharmaceuticals account for 95 percent of McKesson's sales, its health care IT services, such as radiology workstations that give immediate access to medical images from CTs and MRIs, as well as barcode-scanning devices to ensure that medications are administered safely, are also substantial. John Hammergren became CEO in 2001, on the heels of an internal accounting crisis, which put McKesson's reputation in jeopardy. Since then, McKesson has completed numerous acquisitions and revived its brand as part of its vision to help transform health care by increasing patient accessibility, reducing costs, and improving the quality of services and information.

Under Hammergren's strategy of innovative growth and continual process improvement, McKesson's revenues and earnings (excluding one-time charges) have more than doubled to $93 billion and

$913 million, respectively. Compounded over a three-year period (2005, 2006, and 2007), McKesson's total return to shareholders was 28 percent, and its operating earnings increased 15.9 percent. Average return on equity for McKesson during the same three-year period was 14.7 percent. (Source: Standard & Poor's RIWeb.)

At McKesson, employees' rational engagement can be seen in internal data, which show that 87 percent of McKesson's workforce strongly believes in the company's goals and objectives. At a motivational level, 95 percent say they work beyond what is required of them. McKesson's collective employee engagement scores have ranked above industry norms for the past five years.

Hammergren routinely keeps his board of directors informed about the company's engagement levels. "True engagement is earned over time," he told us. "It takes a steadfast emphasis on what is important to us, to our customers, and to our employees."

MGM GRAND HOTEL AND CASINO

A subsidiary of MGM Mirage (one of America's Most Admired Companies for seven consecutive years), Las Vegas–based MGM Grand Hotel and Casino is one of the world's largest resort casinos, with more than 6,772 rooms and almost 10,000 employees. In 2001, President and COO Gamal Aziz took over and spearheaded a $400 million–plus revamp of the property. Today, it houses thirty-six restaurants, bars, nightclubs, and retail outlets. It has received fifty-four AAA Diamond awards (more than any other hotel in the United States, Mexico, and the Caribbean). MGM Grand has also been named a Best Place to Work in Southern Nevada in 2005, 2006, and 2007, and racked up numerous awards for its training, communication, and diversity efforts.

Since Aziz took over, his strategy to make MGM Grand a top

Vegas destination—not just a place to sleep and gamble—has been realized. His efforts to create memorable guest experiences have grown operating profit 68 percent, from $714 million to $1.2 billion, between 2002 and 2007.

Not surprisingly, MGM Grand's thousands of staffers report impressive levels of engagement. More than 90 percent of MGM Grand's employees said they have feelings of respect and dignity; a sense of equity and fairness; and satisfaction with both their jobs and the work environment. Other internal employee measurements reflect employees' passion for MGM Grand's products and services, a key in the hospitality business where stellar customer service is a huge competitive advantage. Specifically, 89 percent of MGM Grand's employees say their work has special meaning; 80 percent say their work is important; and 91 percent are proud to tell others where they work.

Aziz, who was named Nevada's Hotelier of the Year in 2005, puts it simply: "When employees feel good about a company, they give it their all."

NORTH SHORE–LONG ISLAND JEWISH HEALTH SYSTEM

This enormous, multifacility health care system in and outside New York City serves 5.2 million people. The result of mergers of fifteen hospitals and three trauma centers, North Shore–LIJ employs 38,000 people in administration and patient care roles. In 2001, new CEO Michael Dowling spearheaded monumental organizational change to combat high turnover and alarmingly low customer-experience feedback from patients and families. His mission continues to be to make North Shore–LIJ a national health care leader, committed to excellence, compassion, and improving the health of the community. The mission is buttressed by Dowling's emphasis on people-driven process innovation (there's always a better way to do things) and quality service (treat people not just as patients, but as customers who deserve a positive experience).

Between 2001 and 2007, North Shore–LIJ has grown its revenue from $3 billion to $4.5 billion, generating operating gains of almost $57 million in 2007 compared to $35 million in 2001.

Seventy-seven percent of North Shore–LIJ employees described themselves as engaged in their work in 2005, the most recent year North Shore–LIJ surveyed its workforce. Seventy-four percent of employees reported being committed to the organization.

That same year, Dowling received the national Employer of the Year Award from the Employee Services Management Association for his dedication and commitment to an employee-focused culture of excellence. Says Dowling, "Employee engagement automatically leads to better customer satisfaction. Lots of research proves this, but for me it's amazing that people even need research."

Novartis AG

Novartis was formed in 1996 from the combination of two leading Swiss-based pharmaceutical companies, Ciba-Geigy and Sandoz. Today, the Basel, Switzerland–based global health care company provides a portfolio of innovative medicines, generic pharmaceuticals, vaccines, diagnostics, and consumer health products. The seventh-biggest seller of prescription drugs in the United States, Novartis's fifty pharmaceuticals include Diovan, which treats hypertension; Glivec and Zometa for certain cancers; and antifungal agent Lamisil.

Novartis employs approximately 100,000 employees in more than 140 countries. In 2007, it was named *Fortune* magazine's Most Admired Pharmaceutical Company (its fifth year on that list) and was among *Barron's* 100 Most Respected Companies. With a strategic emphasis on innovation and corporate citizenship, Novartis spends approximately 17 percent of its revenues on research and development annually, with some 140 projects currently in its development pipeline. In 2007, Novartis donated $937 million in pharmaceuticals, which reached some 65.7 million patients with diseases such as malaria, tuberculosis, leprosy, and cancer.

Novartis reported record financial results in 2007, with earnings of $11.9 billion on revenues of $39.8 billion. Over the past ten years, Novartis has outperformed its peers in terms of total shareholder return, delivering 9.9 percent compared to its peers' 8.7 percent. Compounded over a three-year period (2005, 2006, and 2007), Novartis's total return to shareholders was 4.3 percent, and its operating earnings increased 3 percent. Average return on equity for Novartis during the same three-year period was 16 percent.

Based on its internal survey, 80 percent of Novartis's top global leaders are characterized as very engaged. The company's additional engagement measurements positively support what Novartis has identified as its most influential engagement drivers: 94 percent of Novartis's global leaders say they have a clear understanding of overall goals and objectives; 93 percent believe the organization is socially responsible in the community; and 91 percent have confidence in decisions made by executive leadership.

Explains Novartis CEO Dr. Daniel Vasella: "An important question to ask is, 'What engages the individual?' . . . [I believe] when people have a sense of usefulness, personal impact, and identify with the mission of the company within society, then they go beyond what they would normally do."

RECREATIONAL EQUIPMENT, INC. (REI)

Founded as a cooperative specializing in outdoor gear, REI positions itself as not just a store, but also a way of life. The retailer's motto sums up its ambition: "We inspire, educate and outfit for a lifetime of outdoor adventure and stewardship." Today, Seattle-based REI has approximately one hundred stores and more than 10,000 employees in the United States. Its growth has come with a unique challenge: staffing stores with people who love the outdoors and love working with people. To maintain its unique competitive advantage, REI's in-store sales force must be made up of inspiring and inspired activity enthusiasts capable of delivering superior customer service.

The privately held REI had sales of $1.3 billion in 2007, up 13.5 percent from 2006, when sales grew another 15 percent from 2005. As a co-op, REI shares profits with members—employees as well as customers—and in 2007, REI distributed $62.8 million to 3.4 million active members.

In 2007, 79 percent of REI's employees were characterized as highly engaged, topping our global retail industry norm of 70 percent engagement. Other findings reflect REI's ability to successfully care for, involve, and inspire its workforce: 80 percent of REI's employee survey respondents feel satisfied with REI as a workplace; 87 percent feel they are part of a team; and 81 percent agreed that management is competent at running the business. In a sign of loyalty and pride, more than 91 percent say they would "gladly refer a good friend or family member for employment." REI has spent eleven consecutive years on *Fortune*'s annual 100 Best Places to Work list.

Sally Jewell joined REI from the banking industry as COO in 2000. She was appointed CEO in 2005. Jewell tells her managers to "start with the premise that you trust employees to want to make the company more effective . . ."

WE'LL MEET employees and leaders from the Engaging Eight throughout this book, as we connect their behaviors with bottom-line results.

A Few Words About Engagement and Strategic Alignment

It's obvious that our Engaging Eight are a diverse group from the perspective of industry, size, geographic footprint, and a host of other factors. At the same time, what connects them is an abiding belief in the power of their people to drive their performance and their own recognition that creating engagement is the job of leaders and managers.

What also connects them is a sophisticated understanding that every engaging workplace is unique in its own right because it has to reflect and reinforce the special needs and competitive priorities of the organization. There is not a one-size-fits-all approach to closing the engagement gap. On the contrary, while there are broad principles and areas for action, as we'll see throughout this book, how those principles and actions are implemented must take shape very differently if they are to have meaning for employees.

What our research and experience clearly illustrate is that engagement efforts start with the organization's strategy and unique basis for competition. Whatever business strategy your company emphasizes—efficiency and cost savings, superior quality, innovation, customer service, or image—workplace practices must reflect and actively drive behaviors to deliver on that strategy and your desired competitive positioning.

A manufacturer competing chiefly on cost and efficiency, for instance, needs to emphasize different employee behaviors than, say, a luxury-goods retailer for which personalized customer attention is the ultimate differentiator. The culture that each organization shapes and sustains—and the investments made in practices and programs that help define the culture—varies considerably.

Data from our *Global Workforce Study* demonstrate the importance of tight alignment across strategy, culture, and workforce programs. What we found is a strong correlation between employees' positive perceptions of their company's ability to compete in their strategic area and the company's ability to support strategically related workplace attributes. In other words, when culture and workplace practices are aligned, the company is well positioned to succeed in employees' eyes and is, in fact, viewed as doing so. By contrast, when culture and practices are not aligned, employees have little confidence in the company's successful execution of its strategy, in part because they themselves don't feel they can do what's required to deliver on the strategy.

For our Engaging Eight, strategic alignment is evident both in how individuals behave and perform and in the overall company results that accrue from the combined efforts of so many people going above and beyond. While your organization's circumstances will not precisely mirror any one of the Engaging Eight, we believe that the insights each of those organizations provides will stimulate you to develop creative approaches that foster higher levels of employee engagement to drive even higher levels of performance.

Once again, our *Global Workforce Study* data provide ample demonstration of this reality: The more engaged people feel, the more they believe they can impact the quality of their company's products and services as well as impact customer satisfaction, revenue growth, costs, overall profitability, and innovation. And the more they believe they can do it, the more likely they are to take positive action to make it happen.

Exhibit C presents stark evidence of this, showing the dramatic differences in the extent to which engaged employees versus the other groups believe they can positively impact performance metrics such as service or product quality, innovation, and costs.

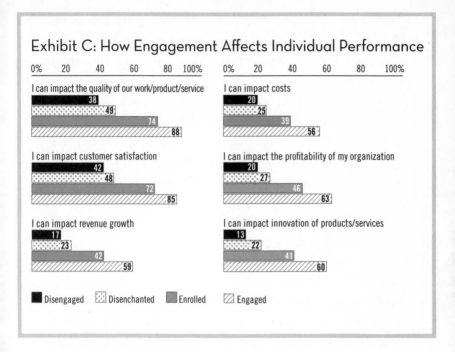

Exhibit C: How Engagement Affects Individual Performance

I can impact the quality of our work/product/service		I can impact costs	
Disengaged	38	Disengaged	20
Disenchanted	49	Disenchanted	25
Enrolled	74	Enrolled	39
Engaged	88	Engaged	56
I can impact customer satisfaction		**I can impact the profitability of my organization**	
Disengaged	42	Disengaged	20
Disenchanted	48	Disenchanted	27
Enrolled	72	Enrolled	46
Engaged	85	Engaged	63
I can impact revenue growth		**I can impact innovation of products/services**	
Disengaged	17	Disengaged	13
Disenchanted	23	Disenchanted	22
Enrolled	42	Enrolled	41
Engaged	59	Engaged	60

■ Disengaged   ▦ Disenchanted   ■ Enrolled   ▨ Engaged

The bottom line: engagement is a key driver of overall organizational performance. When people feel engaged in their work, they tend to work more effectively and more selflessly, take actions that meet customer needs, think creatively, and find innumerable ways to help the company move closer to achieving its vision.

The challenge for you and your company, as for all organizations, is to design workforce strategies and allocate time, management attention, and financial resources to Know, Grow, Inspire, Involve, and Reward employees in ways that support your unique organizational goals and strategies.

And that's precisely what we intend to show you throughout this book.

2

Know Them

DEVELOP WORKFORCE INSIGHT FOR
COMPETITIVE ADVANTAGE

Our management culture values the individual.
—*John Hammergren, CEO, McKesson Corp.*

t can take a crisis to transform the way a company does business, which is exactly what happened to McKesson Corporation in 1999. Three months after the multibillion-dollar health care products and services provider acquired medical software outfit HBOC, an accounting scandal emerged. As a result, McKesson began to buckle. A resulting investigation sapped investors' confidence in McKesson, and nearly half of its market capitalization— $9 billion—evaporated in a single day. In the months that followed, top officers left both HBOC and McKesson in disgrace as customers, employees, and investors questioned the 170-year-old company's integrity.

On the heels of the scandal, the company's returning former chairman and CEO, Alan Seelenfreund, named two seasoned inside executives to lead the company through change and rebuild it. John H. Hammergren and David Mahoney were appointed co-CEOs.

A cornerstone of their comeback plan was to "recover the minds and souls" of McKesson's workers. Many had been devastated both emotionally and financially by the scandal. The stock options previously granted to executives who remained with the company were worthless, and employees' faith in leadership was shot.

Hammergren, who ultimately took the helm as sole CEO in 2001 on the strength of his performance, is a modest Midwesterner who grew up watching his father sell medical supplies. He believed the company needed a fresh infusion of energy and effort from employees. Without that, he doubted it had a future, no matter how strong its competitive strategy. Even if employees remained on the payroll, Hammergren feared they would check out emotionally, leaving them unwilling to do what was required to satisfy demanding and critically important customers.

Hammergren immediately set out to determine what McKesson could do to retain and motivate its dispersed, global population. His approach was straightforward, yet astute: ask *all* McKesson workers what mattered most to them and what would motivate them to excel. The company had surveyed workers before, but never in such a comprehensive and consistent manner and with so much at stake. The 2002 survey marked the first of many times McKesson would research employees' views so holistically. The result? For the first time, C-level executives had an accurate picture of the hearts and minds of the entire workforce, as well as a sense of how McKesson compared to the most high-performing, highly engaged organizations in the country.

This rigorous employee research was part of a widespread cultural and financial transformation at McKesson, and the company continues to monitor the state of the workforce to ensure that executives are engaging employees and to evaluate the company's ongoing progress.

Under Hammergren's strategy of innovative growth and continual process improvement, McKesson's fiscal 2007 revenues and earnings (excluding one-time changes) more than doubled to $93 billion and $913 million, respectively. Compounded over a three-year period (2005, 2006, and 2007), McKesson's total return to shareholders was 28 percent, and its operating earnings increased 15.9 percent. Average return on equity for McKesson during the same three-year period was 14.7 percent. Not coincidentally, McKesson's research indicated that the workforce was also exceptionally engaged in 2008:

- 79 percent would recommend McKesson as a good place to work.
- 87 percent are proud to be part of the business.
- 95 percent say they work beyond what is required of them to help the business succeed.

As McKesson has successfully transitioned from survival to growth mode, it continues to research employees' attitudes, values, and performance levels. To achieve its goal to transform health care by reducing costs and improving efficiency and continue its year-over-year growth, some 32,000 workers must be engaged and willing to expend discretionary effort in its many forms. At McKesson, account managers give discretionary effort by educating themselves about products beyond ones they are responsible for selling. This means that when they ask customers, such as office managers at a doctor's office, about problematic parts of their business, the informed medical supply salesperson can recommend other McKesson services, like billing software, even if the account manager does not receive additional compensation from the sale of the technology. Regional warehouse workers—like pick-n-packers— give discretionary effort when they voice innovative ideas to improve their facilities' operations, as opposed to sticking to and grousing about the status quo. This type of employee input helps secure McKesson's place as a valued vendor with huge customers like CVS and Wal-Mart, which have both named McKesson a Supplier of the Year in 2007 and in previous years.

These engaging acts not only enhance McKesson's business and financial health, but also improve the health and well-being of millions of people who are affected by McKesson's products and services each year.

Develop Workforce Insight for Competitive Advantage

McKesson demonstrates the power that companies gain from truly understanding their workforces and individual workers. John Hammergren and his executive team believe that employee feelings, perceptions, and attitudes are key to driving McKesson's performance, and that a high level of employee engagement is essential to ongoing innovation, collaboration, customer service and, ultimately, business and financial performance.

Understanding what motivates workers to perform—and translating that understanding into actions that successfully motivate them—has always been vital. But in the last twenty-five years, this has become far more important because of dramatic changes in how organizations themselves operate. With few exceptions, the bureaucratic, hierarchical model—where power resides in the hands of a few—has given way to leaner, flatter structures, where disparate and geographically dispersed populations of knowledge workers have more freedom to operate in accordance with shared, company-designed principles, with limited manager oversight. And with individual workers gaining more control over what they do, when they do it, and how they do it, leaders must know even more about what unleashes discretionary effort. And that requires a level of insight into the workforce that is far deeper and more comprehensive than has traditionally been the case.

Certainly, employee surveys are far from new, but historically, they've tended to be simple, often pro forma questionnaires focusing on opinions, the results of which gathered dust on corporate shelves. But over the last decade, something interesting has happened: the sophisticated techniques companies have mastered on the marketing side of the business—tools they use to understand their consumers—have become relevant for employees, ushering in something of a revolution in employee research.

Organizations spend billions of dollars annually on sophisticated, tailored market research to understand, predict, and cater to consumers' behavior, motivations, and values. The most data-driven companies rarely create or launch products without first making sure that those products reflect the conscious and subconscious needs, preferences, and likely buying behaviors of consumers or end users in their target markets. Companies also develop sophisticated individual profiles of their most lucrative customers and can articulate with uncanny precision critical points in the customer life cycle. They know, for example, when an outreach call from a company representative can significantly increase the probability of retaining a customer or selling more services. Advanced analytics and market research—drawn from a deeper knowledge of psychographics and neuroscience, especially the role of emotion in decision making—help give companies the information they need to deliver better customer outcomes and stronger business performance.

Now these research models are being adapted to develop a better understanding of employees' behavior and motivations as well. After all, the same individuals making daily choices about whether to buy Coke or Pepsi, Volvo or BMW, Apple or Dell also choose which company to work for and, once employed, at what level to contribute. Ensuring they make the best choices at every stage of their employment is far from a simple matter since the dynamics behind those decisions mirror the complexities of virtually all human decisions. The good news is that companies can learn from the evolution of consumer research tactics and dive into the science of psychographics—attributes relating to personality, values, attitudes, interests, or lifestyles—to understand the emotional, rational, and motivational drivers of engagement, and what it takes to elicit people's dedication and energy.

Such insight lets senior leaders and midlevel managers articulate characteristics about their workforce with the same certainty that they use to describe the company's core customers. And perhaps, most important, the insights gleaned from employee research and demographic patterns provide a road map of the steps required to engage the workforce and identify the types of workplace investments that will have the greatest impact.

Knowledgeable organizations have a clear picture of the demographics of their workforce. They don't stop at the obvious characteristics like gender, age, and career stage. They also have a good view into the range of performance ratings and promotional potential, turnover and retirement patterns, employee mobility across locations or functions, relevant labor market trends, and a host of related variables. They identify the high potentials being groomed for the roles and positions that have the greatest impact on their financial results, and understand how to keep those people fully engaged. They also have a clear understanding of attitudes across their entire workforce, including national and cultural differences that affect behavior, differences in generational expectations and needs, views about leadership and the company culture, and the attributes that help attract, retain, and engage the type of people most critical to the organization.

At EMC's three-year-old R&D facility in China, for instance, vice general manager Ying Li knows that learning and professional growth is the number one priority for its young hires. This is not so different from the majority of EMC's engineers in the United States, who also want to grow intellectually by being challenged to solve tough problems. In China, however, opportunities to socialize with coworkers outside the office are also tremendously important to young workers. Explains Li, "Here, young engineers want to have fun together and feel like a big family, so we spend a lot of energy on that as well." Li and his managers provide formal group events, like athletic competitions or networking lunches. Satisfying this employee desire also helps EMC execute on its innovation strategy. Says Li, "Our main motivation in China is not to access the most low-cost workers, but to find the best engineers in the talent pool and let them work on EMC's future projects. That really motivates our engineers in China."

On the flip side, consider what happened when EMC did not immediately recognize what was important to engineers it employed in India. Years ago, the company's first impulse was to give its India-based employees routine tasks that U.S. engineers didn't want. "That's the worst thing you can do for bright minds," says Polly Pearson, vice president of EMC's employment brand and engagement strategy. "Smart companies give their global development teams a mix of cutting-edge stuff and legacy systems to work on." Today, EMC does just that. In 2007, *CIO* magazine named EMC one of the top one hundred companies embracing IT innovations, a recognition that could not have been achieved without engaged technologists on staff around the world.

Ultimately, knowledgeable organizations know how to Grow, Inspire, Involve, and Reward their workers, as a group and individually, because they know those workers on both levels with depth and specificity.

Our Engaging Eight companies understand what motivates employees and what types of targeted investments will produce the most tangible returns; for example:

- In retail, employee turnover is a constant challenge and represents a significant direct and indirect cost. Adventure-gear retailer REI has significantly reduced its turnover by providing programs that it knows its employees really want and cannot get from other retailers. From its internal surveys, REI has learned that skill building is very important to its twenty-something population, while employees in their thirties and forties want clear opportunities for career advancement. To satisfy this hunger for growth, REI no longer relies solely on on-the-job training like most retailers, but also offers formal management training and development classes for even its most inexperienced supervisors. When employees "graduate" from required courses, they become "endorsed" and can apply for more senior positions. Results include salespeople and managers who feel well trained and supported, more internal promotions than in years past, as well as lower job-replacement and turnover costs than industry averages.

- At Novartis, employee research has revealed that sales representatives are motivated not just by how much they are paid, but also by the company's level of commitment to corporate citizenship. Novartis allocates significant resources to developing and distributing drugs without charge to in-need populations and makes a point to communicate these efforts to its employees. Novartis also knows its general workforce cares a great deal about patient focus, which is not surprising for people attracted to the health care field. To capitalize on this focus, Novartis is trying to reduce bureaucracy and simplify processes so employees can spend less time on internal activities and more time focusing on patient needs.

- When MGM Grand President Gamal Aziz came on board in 2001 and surveyed employees, the majority complained they didn't know what was going on with the company or at the hotel. Not only did that lack of information make employees feel like outsiders at their own organization, but it also decreased the level of customer service they delivered. How could a games dealer tell a guest what comedian was performing at the amphitheater if the dealer was never told Robin Williams was the headliner? To better inform and involve employees in the hotel's happenings—from revenue growth to high-profile guests they could expect to see roaming the casino floors—Aziz and his staff initiated a daily custom called the Pre-Shift meeting, a ten-minute gathering where group managers review a daily e-mail from MGM Grand's internal communications office that summarizes what is happening in and around the hotel that day. We'll discuss the Pre-Shift in more detail in a later chapter, but suffice it to say for now that today MGM Grand's employees report feeling very involved, and customer service ratings have improved every year under Aziz's leadership.

- Campbell knows that Millennials—workers born around 1980 through 1995—make up approximately 15 percent of its workforce. Unlike many organizations that are not doing anything with this information, Campbell actively teaches its top executives (non-Millennials) what this new generation of workers values. For example, Millennials tend to care more about recognition than their older colleagues. Campbell also provides managers with company-branded thank-you notes to make it easy to show regular appreciation to Millennials, as well as all generations of workers. As we will explore in more detail, even the CEO himself hand-writes hundreds of personal notes to Campbell employees each year. The result is a workforce that feels appreciated.

If you fail—as a manager and as a company—to understand what drives employees' behavior, what makes people tick, and what ticks them off, then you will fail to achieve the maximum return on investment in your people. This, ultimately, will cause you to fall short for customers and investors. A deficit of knowledge about your workforce and individual employees is, at a minimum, a lost opportunity. At worst, it could be tantamount to fiduciary irresponsibility. Quite simply, lack of employee knowledge wastes money and could prevent more money from coming in.

All Workers Are Not Alike: What You Need to Know

The globalization of business has put the last nail in the coffin of the one-size-fits-all workplace. It would be hard to find an organization today that didn't acknowledge the diversity of its population or the changing nature of employees' priorities and needs over the course of their lives and careers. Among employees of varying ages, job functions, and locations, identical policies can result in widely different levels of engagement and patterns of behavior on the job. But acknowledging diversity and shaping a workplace around it are two very different things.

While virtually all companies do recognize the lack of homogeneity in their workforces, many have not yet cracked the code on adapting the workplace. The reason, simply, is that it's very hard. Not only does it require a commitment to continually studying the workforce, it also requires adapting employee practices, policies, and programs to the insights generated from that research.

Our own experience with organizations worldwide—as well as the results from our global research studies over the past decade—reveals profound differences among different groups of workers. There are differences in how people ascribe status, by title or by performance. There are differences in the connotation of corporate responsibility: in the United States, it means environmental and social awareness, while in China, corporate responsibility is more about supporting the state. In some cultures, it is unacceptable to outperform one's boss; we have actually seen individuals hold back on performance so they will not outshine their supervisor. In other regions, meritocracy reigns and front-line managers want direct reports to actively gun for their jobs. In Germany, work and personal life tend to be much more separate than in, say, Spain, where coworkers are much more likely to know about their colleagues' families and hobbies. In many Asian countries, where hierarchies and status are extremely important, workers are much less likely to volunteer ideas in a meeting attended by a superior executive than would be the case in the United States, where it can pay off to impress the boss.

Differences abound within borders as well. Women trying to balance the demands of work and young children are not typically looking for a big career step that would require a lot of global travel. Try them in fifteen years, though, and you often find eager employees with great experience who want to jump to new career levels. More-mature workers often want flexibility to work fewer hours and closer to home. Time and again, we find people want to contribute in different ways—for example, to work on special projects devoted to longer-term issues without the pressure of day-to-day business demands, to establish community relations, or to train new employees. Employees entering the workforce seldom turn down the opportunity to join a company with a great reputation if they have a chance to grow their career there.

How much do you know about your own organization's workforce as well as your direct reports? Test your knowledge by asking yourself the following questions:

TEN THINGS EVERY ORGANIZATION'S SENIOR LEADERS SHOULD KNOW ABOUT THE WORKFORCE

1. How well do employees understand the organization's strategy and embrace the company's core values? Do they believe in the strategy and have confidence that senior leadership has what it takes to achieve it?
2. What percentage of employees know what to do in their jobs to add value to your organization? How many can articulate in specific terms the ways in which their day-to-day activities support the organization's broader strategy and goals?
3. What are the most critical employee retention points in your organization? For example, if people make it past the two-year mark, are they likely to stay at least another ten years?
4. How many of your employees are in retention risk zones? Common zones are the first year of employment, the period after people meet their requirements for early retirement, and periods between seven and ten years of employment for "up-or-out" cultures.
5. How many of your employees are ready for a promotion?

Are expectations for promotion aligned with realistic opportunities? Are people getting adequate preparation and training
to succeed at the next level?

6. How many employees exceed their annual performance goals?
   How many don't? What drives those who do?

7. What rewards have the highest perceived value among each
   workforce segment? How well are rewards aligned with those
   values?

8. For those who recommend the company as a great place to
   work, what do they say are the key reasons?

9. For those who say they are proud of their company, what
   makes them feel this way?

10. Do employees believe that the company delivers on its prom-
    ise to customers? If not, why not?

The prior ten questions focus on key metrics and information to
help you gain insight about the workforce as whole. It's just as
important for people who supervise or manage others to understand
the perspectives and likely behavior of individual employees.

Ten Things Every Front-line Manager Should Know About Individual Employees

1. What aspects of "total rewards" (compensation, appreciation,
   recognition, work-life balance, etc.) are most relevant and
   meaningful to the employees working for you?

2. What are their career expectations? To become a senior executive one day? To remain an individual contributor? Or to make
   their mark in a completely different way?

3. What brought these employees to the company, and what
   keeps them here?

4. How long were these individuals in their prior jobs? What led these individuals to leave their prior employers?

5. When are your employees most likely to be at risk for leaving the company? What sort of outreach will mitigate that risk?

6. What do the people in your group do outside of work, and what's most important to them at the current point in their lives? Family/kids? Hobbies? Socializing?

7. How do these employees view senior management? What actions would demonstrate to them that senior management is interested in their well-being?

8. What things inspire the employees who work for you?

9. What do these employees really want to learn about?

10. What do employees need to know about the business to appreciate their own contributions to overall success?

Answers to many of these questions come through surveys of the workforce. Others can be determined by synthesizing employee data that the organization routinely collects. Still other questions can be answered only by engaging directly in one-on-one conversations. Interestingly, the latter approach can produce some of the best and most actionable insights, but it remains the least common source of information, chiefly because many managers feel ill at ease or ill equipped to have these conversations.

Employers are not the only ones responsible for amassing knowledge. Employees have a responsibility here as well. Below is a companion list of things that every employee should be able to answer about his or her own organization.

TEN THINGS EVERY EMPLOYEE SHOULD KNOW

1. What is the company's primary mission? What are its long-term goals and its values?

2. How is the company performing financially? What were revenues and earnings for the last fiscal year? What is its current market capitalization? How do those numbers compare to competitors?

3. What are the company's greatest competitive challenges at this time? What are the industry's biggest challenges?

4. Who is the CEO, how long has he or she been with the organization, and what is his or her background? Can you answer these same questions for your direct manager and his or her boss?

5. What are the capabilities or skills you must demonstrate in order to move ahead in the organization? What does your manager see as your greatest strengths and most limiting weaknesses?

6. What is your intended or desired career path over the next two years, and is it clear to you how to get on that path in your organization?

7. What formal education and learning opportunities does your employer make available to you? Which ones are most relevant to help you advance to your next desired career level?

8. What socially responsible activities does your company undertake? How can you help the organization be a better corporate citizen?

9. How does your work contribute to the company's business goals? Do you understand how your daily activities and decisions affect the organization?

10. Can you articulate what factors go into determining your over-

all compensation and what factors contribute most to determining your bonus or next salary increase? Are you familiar with all the health and financial benefits your company offers?

If you don't know the answers to every one of these questions, find out. The knowledge will help make you a more productive and engaged employee.

MACRO AND MICRO KNOWLEDGE

There are two levels of knowledge that every organization—and every manager—must have regarding their workforce:

MACROLEVEL KNOWLEDGE: Understanding demographics and trends for the overall workforce and large subgroups.

MICROLEVEL KNOWLEDGE: Understanding individual workers and what specifically motivates them.

Macro knowledge is a working grasp of the workforce's overall profile—its demographic makeup—as well as an understanding of workforce segments, whether segmented by age (Baby Boomers vs. Millennials), job category (salespeople vs. scientists), or geographic location (Beijing vs. North Carolina). Demographic knowledge includes knowing what percentage of the workforce is composed of new college graduates or how many workers have young children or aging parents. Organizational knowledge includes things like the number of new hires brought in annually and why they joined; the number of employees leaving each year and why; changes in what people value most from the organization and their rewards package; and how much they buy into the company's mission and trust its leaders.

Because of McKesson's employee research, CEO John Hammergren, his HR professionals, and direct managers can articulate what drives their workforce at a macro level. First and foremost, they know their workforce has a strong belief in the company's stated goals and objectives, as well as a clear understanding of objectives at the departmental level. Together, these factors carry twice as much weight with workers as the next employee priority: career development. Sixty-eight percent of McKesson workers want opportunities for personal development and growth, as well as a colleague who personally encourages their own growth and development. Still another key driver of engagement at McKesson is "management leadership." Specifically, employees want their managers to make fair decisions about employee-related matters. These attributes—belief in the company goals, opportunities for career development, and fair decision making—inform where and how McKesson allocates resources.

For example, one way McKesson keeps employees rallied and informed around its mission is via Hammergren's quarterly employee calls the morning after the company announces earnings to Wall Street. "Part of what we discuss is our financial performance, and the view of our performance against competitors, and what we are doing with major customers," he says. Hammergren also takes questions from the employees listening in on the call. Says Hammergren, "People are not shy about what they will ask, and I think we get some credit for being very willing to stand up and take those [tough] questions." Similarly, Hammergren holds "town hall" meetings at large regional offices. Each year he tries to meet with as many employees as possible in person. Again, he always articulates the company's agenda and takes unsolicited questions from people.

Macro knowledge also helps identify the type of person most likely to thrive in a specific corporate culture. Someone with an entrepreneurial mind-set, for example, will likely be more engaged in a nonhierarchical environment. As Honeywell's vice president of communications, Tom Buckmaster, told us about his company's workforce, "We know that the kind of people who are successful here are those who are comfortable with ambiguity . . . you need stamina to work here and it is not for the faint of heart . . . there is an intensity about the performance culture that is not right for everyone." In this way, macro knowledge informs hiring decisions, helping managers focus on candidates that match the temperament and experience of an organization's most successful employees.

Hiring the right people on the front end does not ensure their engagement over the long term; even the most self-motivated and talented individuals can be encouraged or discouraged to give their all. But investing the time to carefully screen for a close cultural match at the outset certainly makes engagement more likely later on.

ORGANIZATIONAL, WORK EXPERIENCE, AND INTRINSIC EFFECTS ON ENGAGEMENT

Going a bit deeper, companies and managers must also understand how the organization itself, employees' work experience, and employees' own personalities and natures affect their relationship to the company and their likely level of engagement and performance. Let's consider each in turn:

THE ORGANIZATION: Company-wide practices, senior leadership behaviors, and the general work environment that affect employees' perceptions of their work experience.

THE WORK EXPERIENCE: The day-to-day, local experience an employee has, his interaction with front-line managers, and the unique factors influencing his daily activities.

THE INTERPERSONAL: An individual's traits and personal orientation that affect her perceptions of the job and her inclination to take on additional responsibilities.

Recall our ten global drivers of engagement, which cross these basic categories. Perhaps the most compelling finding from our *Global Workforce Study* is that the organization, not the daily work experience or an employee's personality, has the greatest influence on engagement. Note back in chapter 1, where we introduced the drivers of engagement, just how pervasive the organization's influence actually is. Five of the top ten drivers of engagement globally tie to the organization itself. Only three are related to the daily work experience. And just two—setting high personal standards and enjoying challenge on the job—are intrinsic aspects of an individual's character and personality.

This is good news for leaders because it runs counter to the widely held view that engaged employees are born, not developed. And it confirms that focusing on company practices and programs is anything but a waste of time. In fact, while a person's traits certainly contribute to his or her level of engagement, over time a company can drive that level up or down dramatically, depending on the environment it creates and sustains.

While companies don't have to rely on finding people who are "born engaged," it is nonetheless true that interpersonal traits do come into play in influencing engagement. These include a person's values, cultural background, work ethic, level of ambition, even family responsibilities. Does an industrial engineer value ongoing education over pay? To what degree does a salesperson hold herself accountable to high-performance standards?

We see organizational and interpersonal dynamics at play at technology services firm EMC, where product quality is paramount because defects in EMC's complex storage software products could mean the loss of millions of dollars for a client. EMC's high-performance culture is known for attracting ambitious self-starters. That inner drive is compounded by an organizational factor: high expectations from peers—not just from direct bosses—that further induce people to put in extra effort and excel so they will not let their colleagues down. Some EMCers describe this cultural dynamic as a sort of peer pressure to perform, and—like an Olympic team going for the gold—it proves an engaging force in its own right.

Understanding the combination of organizational, work experience, and interpersonal factors that affect the workforce as a whole and the individuals who comprise the workforce requires a trio of research approaches:

- Face-to-face interactions between leaders and workers.
- Employee surveys.
- Workforce metrics.

Engaging companies—and engaging managers—synthesize information from these three sources to draw inferences and develop rich insight about employees to determine how to best invest money, time, and energy into the workforce.

LISTEN TO THE CACOPHONY: FACE-TO-FACE INTERACTIONS

There is no substitute for personal touch. One-on-one "research" reveals insights about individual workers that a formal survey often misses, mainly interpersonal drivers at the micro level.

Engaging bosses make conscious efforts to learn what's important to individuals, especially high performers and high-potential employees. Knowing workers is not about getting overly personal and becoming friends. What is required, however, is the same level of knowledge, understanding, and insight that the best athletic coaches have about players on their teams. They take the time to understand their players' individual motivations and understand what drives their desire to perform their best.

It is important to get to know workers through conversations in addition to data, but let the latter inform the former. This responsibility usually falls to direct managers—from the CEO to line supervisors—who must call upon their communication skills, intuition, and experience to determine the combination of drivers that engage their people—especially the most valuable contributors. Indeed, at the height of McKesson's crisis, co-chief Hammergren left the corporate headquarters and visited with hundreds of employees to explain what had happened and articulate what the future might hold. In turn, he heard what workers had to say. He listened to their concerns as well as their professional desires.

There is no substitute for the one-on-one conversation as a tool to understand what drives individual workers. Engaging managers use what they hear to guide employees toward company programs, such as outside education opportunities, and to inform their own daily management style.

Getting to know people is not an easy task. Each manager must find his or her own sincere style and cultivate what may not come naturally. Leaders at our Engaging Eight companies dedicate time to getting to know employees on a personal basis. Some invite them to dinner; others embark on town hall meetings. There is no universal ideal way to go about this, and anecdotes provide some of the approaches that have worked for others.

At Honeywell International, CEO Cote explains how and what he learned about Honeywell's non-U.S. technology workers during a trip to India:

> Some years ago, I attended a big dinner in India and I sat down with some workers, and I said, "So, what is it that keeps all of you here? The [employee] band? The cricket team? The community outreach? The scholarships?" They said, "No, every [company] does that stuff!" "Really? Well what keeps you here?" I asked. They told me that, unlike other places, they were given a lot of responsibility. They did not always have to check in with people, and they were given a package of work that became their responsibility. "It's up to us to get it done," they said. "And, if we have an issue or need advice, we can go right to the head of the operation and ask him . . . he will talk with us and he will work with us."

To help workers open up about themselves, the boss can open up about him- or herself. Days after Doug Conant joined Campbell, he spent an hour alone with each senior executive and shared with him or her "an extensive amount of information" about himself. Says Conant:

> At the most senior levels, work is a very large part of your life. People are looking to do more than make a living. They want to leave a legacy of contribution that they and their families

can feel good about. To get on that track, I've found that it's important to get started working together, in a deeper-than-average, more personal way. Typically, the first hour of the first day we work together, I share an extensive amount of information about myself. I explain that my goal is to take the mystery out of our relationship in a personal way as quickly as possible so that we can get on with the business of working together and doing something special. Too often earlier in my career, I experienced extended periods of time working for a manager that I didn't adequately understand, and it got in the way of my ability to perform.

In the meetings, I explain that I have found a better way to start, at least for me. So, I typically start each one of these conversations by saying, "Over the next hour or so, I will tell you everything you might want to know about me—what's important to me both in and out of work, what I look for in an organization, how I operate, why I do what I do, and much more. At the end of the hour you should have a pretty clear picture of what I'm all about and where I'm headed. Then, if I do what I say I'm going to do, I guess you can trust me. If I don't, I guess you can't. But at least we will know, and we can start moving forward. I'm betting that you will quickly see that I will do what I say I will do, that you can trust me, and that we can do special things together."

At the end of the hour, I invite them to schedule an hour to share their story with me in as much detail as they are comfortable.

Conant, who used the technique prior to joining Campbell, says about half of the executives come back and share details about how they operate and what they want to accomplish personally as well as professionally. As a result, Conant has the information he needs to accommodate their nature and circumstances. While Conant was working at Nabisco, one of his direct reports revealed that he was going through a divorce, and it was important for him to be available and present for his two sons after the family's painful breakup. The executive asked Conant for a flexible schedule to help him manage the situation. "We created a flex schedule for him," recalls Conant, "and I have to tell you, our company got as much from this individual as anyone could have ever gotten from him." At Campbell, one executive Conant interviewed for a position had a dream of sailing across the Atlantic with his father at some point in his career. He told Conant that if he took the job eventually he would need to take a month or so to do it. Conant agreed to make it work, and a few years later the executive did, indeed, make the trip. This individual went on to make many substantial contributions to Campbell.

When President Gamal Aziz joined MGM Grand, his efforts to get to know the workforce included open-ended, face-to-face meetings with small groups of workers. "I would sit with a combination of people from different departments, and we would have breakfast and talk about whatever was on their minds," he recalls. To encourage candid conversations, Aziz asked bosses not to attend the meetings. When he asked employees to tell him what they liked and did not like about their departments, he guaranteed them confidentiality. Says Aziz, "For some reason, if you feel you are going to talk to the president directly, there is a sense of freedom because that person is not your direct supervisor and judgment is not going to be placed."

The head of REI's flagship Seattle store, Rachel Ligtenberg, knows the names of most of the store's 442 employees. Says Ligtenberg, "I want to use their names when I see them in the hall. I do not have tricks, just genuine interest in knowing people and something about them, what they like about the company, where they worked before . . ." It makes a difference. According to at least one of her employees, Duy Tran, who worked for Ligtenberg for four years, one of Ligtenberg's strengths is that "she knows employees really well."

He's adopted his former boss's management style. Says Tran, "Every employee is different, so I invest time in conversation. You just have to open your door and approach them. Otherwise, you play a guessing game about what people want."

Track the Reality of Experience

An important tenet in behavioral science is that people don't always have a good grip on what really makes them behave the way they do. Self-reported preferences are not as reliable as statistically derived preferences. For example, many people might say they would leave a company because of pay. But analyzing data from employees who quit may reveal that they left out of frustration with their ability to balance work with other personal demands. For a company, this analysis implies that it could be far more productive to enable work-life balance than to give everyone a raise. Leaders who really want to know their workforce and their workers will track the reality of experience using surveys, analytic assessments of internal employee data, and workforce metrics.

As a tool, the best surveys borrow from the methods used in market research to capture subjective consumer preferences. When administered and analyzed effectively, engagement surveys in particular can provide a reliable barometer of the workforce's collective state of mind: perceptions about the company, the company's mission, and its leadership.

In effect, surveys (because of their anonymity) are like sanctioned eavesdropping. The results provide insight into how willing workers are to contribute more without being asked or ordered to do so. Surveys tell us how workers think and feel about their company at a given point in time. When surveys are translated into actions, they give senior leaders, human resource professionals, and managers at all levels an understanding of where engagement drivers fall short and what they can do to foster employees' highest levels of engagement and performance within budgetary or other constraints.

Another source of insight from employee surveys is the open-ended survey question. Carefully designed questions can elicit a wealth of information and serve as a kind of virtual focus group for managers. For example, organizations can ask employees for suggestions to improve the company's business or to enhance the effectiveness of a specific department. There is wisdom in crowds, meaning the collective insights of employees can be mined to isolate the best specific ideas for business improvement.

Many managers are tempted to eschew research and simply look for a universal silver bullet that consistently yields engagement. But there isn't one. For every company, for every employee group within the organization, for every individual, there is a unique combination of engagement drivers, and each driver has a different level of importance. That may sound overwhelming, but the goal for an organization and for individual managers is to know the combination of drivers that will be effective for particular employee segments within their workforce. For example, we know from our research and experience that engineers as a professional group—regardless of who they work for—will generally not be engaged unless they can keep their skills up-to-date. EMC, for example, knows its engineers want to work on hot new technologies and has devised ways for them to do so. We also know that high performers must believe that the organization is going in the "right direction" and be able to relate to the company's vision and strategy. But helping employees keep skills up-to-date and clearly communicating vision and strategy might not be engagement drivers for other workforce segments. This notion bears repeating: the degree to which any one engagement driver matters to different people and different work groups inevitably varies.

Employee Research 101

Companies opt to take the pulse of employees in a variety of ways. Recall, for example, how Honeywell International surveys employees who listen to CEO Dave Cote's company-wide one-hour broadcasts at the end of each fiscal quarter. Most of the Engaging Eight organizations survey employees annually to determine their engagement levels and to identify what is most important to the workforce. Engagement surveys mine the psyche, drilling into the hearts and minds of workers. For more detail about what constitutes a successful employee engagement survey, please refer to Exhibit D.

Another effective means to capture detailed insights about worker perceptions and opinions is through live focus groups (facilitated meetings with up to twenty employees). Focus groups allow you to probe ideas and dig into root causes of behavior on the spot. Their drawback is that focus groups are not, generally, statistically representative, mostly because an organization can't afford to talk to that many people, and because the data being captured are qualitative. That said, focus groups do allow companies to explore sensitive subjects in more depth than a survey might allow, provide for a greater level of involvement, and offer an opportunity to manage important messages from the company.

Exhibit D: Engagement Surveys

Ten Golden Rules for Engagement Survey Success

1. **Measure what matters.** To learn what most drives engagement in your organization, design a survey that tests a comprehensive array of items spanning organizational, work experience, and intrinsic personal factors. Narrowing the scope of the survey to the survey designer's favorite topics can provide misleading data.

2. **Encourage voluntary participation by a valid representation of the workforce.** Depending on the size of your population and statistical confidence levels and intervals, you may find that participation as low as 20 percent is statistically valid. However, try to get 100 percent of the workforce to participate. The more people who respond make the findings more acceptable to anyone who looks at them. To encourage broad participation, communicate and formally promote the timing, purpose, and methodology for the survey. Provide ample time—about two to three weeks—for people to complete the survey, and send reminders to generate the highest response levels possible.

3. **Allow for easy access and understanding.** Design and deliver a survey that is easy for all employees to access, understand, and complete, regardless of where they work. Each question should be concise and should not incorporate subquestions. Most surveys ask for degrees of agreement with statements about the company, the employee's work experience, as well as views of managers and leadership initiatives.

4. **Focus on issues that will make a difference to the company's success or the employee's work experience.** You should be sure to include questions about those issues on which you are prepared to act. Even though this approach leaves you open to the risk that you will miss some important input, the alternative poses even more significant risks.

Ten Golden Rules for Engagement Survey Success
(continued)

If you ask questions about sensitive issues that you know you will not address now or in the near future, there is a high likelihood that you will generate unnecessary dissension and skepticism within the workforce.

5. **Emphasize confidentiality.** Be clear with employees about how the data will and will not be used. Explain how confidentiality is guaranteed. Every worker must believe a simple truth: no one at the company—not the boss, not the CEO—will ever know how individual employees answered survey questions.

6. **Analyze employee survey scores in the context of comparative data.** Engagement scores become meaningful when compared to a company's past performance, to engagement levels at other organizations, and to statistically reliable "norms." Among the most effective norms are those derived from companies with both high engagement levels *and* stellar financial results. Smart companies benchmark their engagement scores against these so-called high-performing company norms for a very simple reason. They want to hold themselves to the highest standard of performance across the board—from financial performance to employee engagement.

7. **Share survey insight quickly and with candor.** Postsurvey communication of results is essential. Employee support will wane—and current engagement levels drop—if people hear little or nothing about the results and next steps once the survey has closed. Share the findings—the positive and the negative—with the executive team within a few weeks of the survey's conclusion and with employees as soon as possible after that. Finally, negative results should not be hidden or spun, especially given that the purpose of a survey is to identify priority areas for improvement.

8. **Act on survey results at the corporate level.** Senior management, including the CEO, should review survey results and identify a limited number of company-wide actions that will address pressing

Ten Golden Rules for Engagement Survey Success
(continued)

employee concerns *and* have the potential to drive organizational strategy and results.

9. **Act on survey results at the local level.** Department and group leaders should receive departmental survey results in a manner that guarantees individual employee confidentiality while allowing local leaders to better understand what drives their direct reports and where engagement is falling short. Supplement survey data with material that coaches managers about how to discuss and act on results.

10. **Broadcast the changes.** Down the road, when specific steps are taken as a direct result of survey data, tell employees so they can see the connection between their input and company actions. Don't assume employees will see a link between the survey results and, say, a change in benefit plans or a flextime option. Managers must make the connection for them.

This approach played a key role at McKesson's Carol Stream, Illinois–based distribution center, which distributes $250 million worth of products to 1,100 regional industrial customers, including hospitals. The center's manager, Joe Farrell, was charged with improving the center's performance. As part of his effort he initiated what he called Focus Meetings, biweekly gatherings where representatives from the facility's warehouse, office, and management teams met to discuss issues of concern to employees, and to improve communication between management and workers.

"The idea was not only to listen to their concerns, but to act upon issues raised," Farrell explained in a company newsletter. "When employees started to see that we would follow through with changes they suggested, that went a long way toward building trust." At one meeting, an employee observed that the distribution center did not recognize employees for extraordinary effort. In response, Farrell established a recognition program that provided coins to employees recognized for outstanding performance. The coins can be redeemed for DVDs, shirts, and jackets. In spring 2007, the Carol Stream facility had improved its internal ranking from eighteen to thirteen (out of thirty centers) and received a most-improved distribution center award. This is a terrific example of how local managers can come to know what's on their employees' minds, then act on what they learn.

Another kind of employee data, workforce metrics, provide a view of collective behavior not revealed through surveys. Workforce metrics include information about turnover, retention trends, promotion patterns, hiring patterns, and broad demographic developments.

For example, analyzing data about outgoing employees can reveal if there's a common denominator in departures. If management knows how turnover patterns compare to others in the industry, they can better identify and prevent the problem. One call center operation suffered debilitating turnover of 200 percent—among the worst in its industry. A combination of engagement data and details about management practices brought a curious situation to light. To save money, the center's management had created rotating work spaces, rather than assigning specific desks to every employee. Employees were moved around every day, depending on work schedules and available spaces. But this practice had a negative impact on workers, who had no sense of a home base; the office failed to create a sense of community. The turnover costs resulting from the negative effects of this "hot desking" far outweighed the cost savings of fewer desks.

Workforce metrics can unveil other important insights, like

spikes in turnover, which can then help determine root causes. A spike in attrition at three months might suggest that the company's assimilation program wasn't sufficient. A spike in attrition at five years might suggest that people were staying on not because they were engaged in their work, but because they wanted access to their profit-sharing accounts, which vested at that time. Finding attrition spikes and unearthing their causes will enable organizations to better understand how to keep employees engaged at all points during their employment life cycle.

Organizations should also measure company practices in comparison to employee expectations. One important metric is the gap between actual promotions and employees' expectations for career advancement. An organization might find that people in accounting spend, on average, three years at the entry level, but that entry-level accountants recruited from top colleges expect to be promoted within two years. This one-year discrepancy could explain existing attrition or disengagement of accountants, or alert management to the risk of turnover. Organizations can use metrics to determine whether promotion rates are aligned with employees' expectations for advancement across every major work-force segment.

Companies should also understand how many and what percentage of employees move across the company into another function, business segment, or country. Why might such data be illuminating? Suppose you knew that less than 1 percent of the workforce had the opportunity for a cross-company transfer and less than half of those employees actually made a move. These data are interesting but become even more powerful when considered alongside the fact that over half of the people employed at your company are interested in developing new skills. This gap means the organization is missing an important avenue to meet employees' needs and, as a result, improve retention and engagement of the workforce.

It's also important to examine prospective staffing needs and relevant external labor market conditions. How many people is your organization going to hire this year? Next year? The year after? Are these people—potential employees—available in the regions where they'll be needed? If there's a shortage of people or key skills, what are the options available? Will you need to recruit from other locations? How will that impact your costs? What changes may be required in your rewards package to ensure that you attract whatever talent is available and keep the people you already have?

Given the labor shortages predicted for a variety of industries, every organization needs to understand its hiring challenges relative to the available supply of talent to ensure it doesn't inadvertently find itself with a group of disenchanted or disengaged employees who would be susceptible to advances from other employers.

Workforce insights developed through surveys and comparative metrics help management create composites of collective workforce behavior and define actions the organization must take. That said, insights alone do not move the needle on engagement or create positive change.

Applying Workforce Insight

Get to know your employees, then act accordingly.

In a global marketplace that competes aggressively for top talent, no one can afford to take a scattershot approach with regard to what policies and programs will truly engage workers. Every organization has its own ideal mix that, within budgetary constraints, can yield higher levels of engagement and quantifiable performance results. But it's impossible to capture workers' hearts and minds (unless by luck or accident) if you do not truly understand what will capture both heart *and* mind.

Ultimately, each organization has an optimal portfolio of employee programs that align with its leadership objectives, performance targets, competitive positioning, budget, and employee demographics and preferences. Annual survey results will refine that portfolio.

The question then, is, What to act on?

Not every insight requires action, even areas that received "low" engagement scores. The point isn't to be outstanding in every single aspect of the employment deal. That's neither practical nor affordable. High-performing organizations analyze employee preferences and attitudes in the context of key business issues, and target the two to three initiatives that promise the greatest return. Experience shows that management has the bandwidth to embark on up to four areas of improvement or initiatives each year. Two or three is actually preferable. So what's worth fixing?

At a company-wide level, return can be measured in additional revenue, increased customer loyalty, lower unwanted turnover, as well as higher retention rates of top performers and workers in areas where the labor supply is particularly low. To prioritize, focus actions on employees who are the most critical to the organization. All workers should ideally be engaged, but to optimize engagement efforts, companies should invest more in workers with mission-critical roles. For example, organizations with customer-centric strategies must know what drives its customer-facing employees and, in turn, adjust programs and policies to deliver on those drivers.

Knowing which employees have the most direct impact on performance and profitability—and which jobs are the most critical to the company's strategy—helps target actions and investments. One approach to identify the most critical employees is to group employees into four broad categories, as suggested by John W. Boudreau in his book *Beyond HR: The New Science of Human Capital:*

- *Strategic employees* hold jobs whose outcome directly affects the company's main strategy.
- *Core employees* also affect company strategy, although not as directly.
- *Support employees* are those who the organization cannot do without, but whose value may be realized through less expensive alternative staffing arrangements, such as outsourcing.
- *Noncore employees* no longer align with the company's strategic direction and may need to be retrained or redeployed.

While segmentation informs large-scale programs and policies, managers should focus on getting to know each person in their group and figure out what "deal" will most engage and retain them.

In the next four chapters—Grow, Inspire, Involve, and Reward—we'll discuss specific ways to act on various engagement drivers. Some of the methods and philosophies may already be a significant part of your organization, while others will be new solutions that can help close your own engagement gap and, ultimately, improve overall performance. As long as the actions you take, as an organization and as a boss, are informed by truths you come to know about your workforce and individual employees, they will yield results.

In Closing: The Known Employee

Recall what McKesson's research revealed as two primary engagement drivers among its employees. First, they want to believe in the company's overall goals and objectives and have a clear understanding of them at the departmental level. Second, employees want opportunities for personal development and growth. Having understood these two significant workforce requirements, McKesson has acted in a number of ways that we'll examine in more detail throughout the book. For now, we can see proof that knowing what's important to its workforce has paid off for McKesson.

For example, according to the company's 2008 employee pulse survey, 87 percent of McKesson's employees believe strongly in the goals and objectives of the business. On an individual level, the sentiment is equally strong. Todd Baldanzi is vice president of finance for Moore Medical, a company McKesson acquired in April 2004. At the time, the Connecticut-based Moore had $140 million in revenues and was losing money. Today, sales are growing at double-digit rates annually, and the company had double-digit profit margins in 2007. Baldanzi worked for Moore prior to the acquisition, and below he describes why he has stayed with McKesson since the change in ownership. Note that his reasons reflect what McKesson *knows* are most important to its workforce as a whole: a belief in the company's overall goals and objectives, and opportunities to grow.

McKesson has done a good job laying out a vision statement—improved quality and reduced costs in health care in America. Before McKesson, Moore was always trying new strategies. It's easy from a big-picture perspective to stand back and say, "I feel good about what it is we are doing as a company and each of us is doing a small piece of that." When you know what you need to do, you can focus on it. In the twelve quarters since we were acquired, we have not missed our financial objectives.

As a supervisor, Baldanzi has also translated the company's vision at a local level, helping to engage his direct reports:

> Our job as managers is to help our employees understand that we are playing an important role in the health care supply chain. Success is not just about making sure we get the invoice stamped correctly, but about patients . . . you are able to get through a lot of the day-to-day minutiae when you say, "What about the customer, what about the patient?" McKesson has done a good job of crafting the vision for me. The more my workers get a sense of urgency of how McKesson makes a difference in the world, the better we work.

At thirty-four, Baldanzi adds that he is "young enough that he wants more responsibility and growth" and "the ability to keep moving up at a rate that is faster than normal." Every time he raises his hand to take on additional responsibilities, McKesson listens and gives him the freedom to challenge himself and the power to make decisions quickly. When we spoke, Baldanzi was also acting as Moore's interim head of technology, a position he asked to assume in addition to his regular responsibilities, and without a salary increase. The on-the-job learning has paid off for Baldanzi as well as McKesson, who recently promoted him to the position of chief financial officer at another business unit. Baldanzi will leave Moore in a few months. Meanwhile, he continues to arrive at work early and stay late. "I do it because I want to," he says, "not because I have to."

3

Grow Them

FOSTER LEARNING AND SET CAREER PATHS WITH PURPOSE AND PERSONALIZATION

Big successes are a result of thousands of little things.
—Michael Dowling, President and CEO, North Shore–
Long Island Jewish Health System

hen Michael J. Dowling became president and CEO at one of the nation's largest nonprofit health care systems in 2002, the organization was a complex, unwieldy, inefficient beast. The result of a 1997 merger of two competing health care facilities, North Shore–Long Island Jewish Health System, based in Great Neck, New York, consisted of 27,000 employees at fourteen different hospitals and other health care institutions that served 5.2 million people in the New York City boroughs of Queens and Staten Island, and throughout Long Island.

With an annual budget of about $3 billion, the institution was plagued with problems that stunted the hospitals' effectiveness and prevented health care workers from delivering a consistently positive experience for patients.

North Shore–LIJ's prior problems included very high employee attrition, unacceptable numbers of open positions, and alarmingly low patient satisfaction scores. The organization seemed to lose sight of patients' interests, coming up woefully short on satisfaction and efficiency levels.

All this was happening at the very time patient expectations were rising. Improvements in consumer education and information led people throughout the United States to expect top-quality health care, access to the latest technology, and fewer hassles about insurance reimbursements. What's more, the government and insurers were not reimbursing hospitals enough to cover their costs, and a national shortage of nurses and allied health professionals was also taking a toll. North Shore–LIJ patients were complaining, and the system could not meet its budget. Competition was also intense. The individual institutions composing North Shore–LIJ competed not only with New York City's world-class hospitals for health care workers and patients, but also with one another.

Enter Dowling, a native of Limerick, Ireland, and a former commissioner of health and human services for New York State. He's the type of health care leader drawn more to people than to science, finance, or technology. He prefers to walk the halls and talk to employees face-to-face rather than communicate via e-mail. Not surprisingly, Dowling's plan for creating a united, world-class, and profitable health care system hinged on growing people—not in numbers, per se, but in their abilities.

His strategy was, and continues to be, to foster a workforce comprising people who, in his words, are "not satisfied doing things the way they had always been done." To succeed, Dowling believes people at all levels have to feel motivated and free to question the status quo *and* be capable of improving it. Achieving such a dramatic shift in employee attitude and ability was a daunting task when he joined the organization.

While other leaders might have opted to replace scores of clinical, administrative, and support staffers with new hires, Dowling had a different agenda. At the heart of his plan was creating a culture of continuous learning. He wanted to arm the existing workforce with management tools and knowledge that allowed them to "release the creative ideas they had inside of them" and "increase their capacity, intellect, and skills to initiate change and meet the new demands of the marketplace." Skeptics thought he was spouting management jargon and would not succeed, but he gained credibility as he invested the organization's funds and his own personal energy into programs and behaviors that enhanced North Shore–LIJ's workers' capabilities. This is giving employees a renewed sense of value and passion for their work.

Slowly but surely, staff have begun to come forth with ideas to eliminate the bureaucracy, rather than letting the bureaucracy beat them down. They find little ways to make patients feel they are, indeed, getting the best care possible, and they pay more attention to families, thanks to a newfound understanding that a patient's parents, spouse, siblings, and children are also "customers" of the hospital. All these changes translate into a more efficient, professional, and friendly experience for people who visit all of North Shore–LIJ's member hospitals.

Since 2002, Dowling's continuous-learning mandate has spurred ongoing improvement throughout the health care facilities. For patients, there are shorter wait times when people are transferred from one department to another. Turnaround times for laboratory and radiology results have improved. Family and friends receive great service at the cafeterias. And employees experience faster response times from HR professionals when they call with benefit inquiries. In addition to winning numerous awards, three of the system's hospitals were voted "the most preferred" for their respective counties.

Five years ago, North Shore–LIJ had to look outside to fill almost every vacant position. Today that's rare. What's more, it enjoys a 96 percent employee retention rate, and vacancy rates for critical-care nurses have plummeted, almost unheard of in health care. With its now $4.5 billion operating budget, North Shore–LIJ is one of the Northeast's few profitable health care systems and the third-largest nonprofit, secular health care system in the country. Still, Dowling insists that North Shore–LIJ has a long way to go to be all that it can be. "It's a journey," he says.

In the health care industry, where serious shortages of critical skills continue, learning and development is a key element in driving overall business success. Organizations in health care and similarly labor-challenged industries must rely heavily on skill building and training to meet core talent and workforce needs. North Shore–LIJ's evolution not only underscores this point but also shows the power that growing people has on boosting performance: a learning culture helps ensure that employees have the right skills and knowledge to further the business objectives that drive financial growth.

The impact of learning on the people-performance link is not limited to health care, of course, and far-sighted organizations and their leaders understand the long-term, bottom-line value in creating a culture of continuous learning.

Foster Learning and Education

North Shore–LIJ's learning culture exemplifies one of the key elements that drive employee engagement: growth.

> Workers across industries want short- and long-term opportunities to improve their skills and capabilities so they can increase their marketability, career options, and on-the-job focus and challenges.

Harking back to the top ten global engagement drivers from our *Global Workforce Study*, three of the drivers are embedded in this notion:

- The opportunity an employee has to improve skills and capabilities.
- Excellent career advancement opportunities.
- An individual's interest in challenging work assignments.

On an individual level, the right learning opportunities can engage a worker's heart and mind. People want to grow, and with good reason. The learning process simultaneously stimulates the intellect and elicits feelings of pride and stability. People feel more secure in their ability to compete successfully in the labor force; on the job, they feel far more engrossed in the moment, energetic and useful.

On a global level, a powerful combination of demographic and business trends is focusing more attention on corporate-sponsored learning and development activities. Unrelenting economic pressures—tightening labor pools, rapid technological advancement, increased global competition—combined with declining birthrates in developed countries, increasing life expectancies, and the impending retirement of the Baby Boomer workforce, has sparked important shifts in the labor force. Companies will need to provide new learning and development opportunities to address the resulting skilled-labor shortages.

Organizations are not blind to these global needs and individual preferences—and corporate training efforts are on the rise. According to the American Society for Training and Development (ASTD), the average learning expenditure per employee grew from $799 in 2001 to $1,040 in 2006, a gain of about 30 percent.

The notion that continuous learning can increase employee engagement and, in turn, improve performance may seem clear enough. However, companies are not sufficiently acting on this idea, according to the respondents in our global study. Specifically:

- 36 percent of employees feel they have *not* improved their skills and capabilities over the past year.
- 48 percent say they have *not* received the training they need to do their job effectively.
- A significant majority, 64 percent, believe that their company rates "average" or "below" others in terms of training opportunities.
- 72 percent believe other organizations do a better job than their current employer when it comes to career development.

The message is clear: employers must do a better job training and educating the workforce by putting the right organizational and individual learning elements in place to simultaneously further the growth goals of both the business and individual workers. The right three components—customized for each company—are visible leadership commitment and support, clear purpose, and personalization for individual employees. These three elements must be present at both the organizational and the managerial levels. This means that the CEO, human resources, in-house training professionals, and direct supervisors all have a role in fostering a culture of learning.

But the most important person in the learning equation is the employee. Most people bring a natural inclination for challenge and stimulation to their work. Many of us are born with it and continue to feed that need throughout our lives, especially when it is encouraged in our professions. And indeed, data from our global study confirm this: 83 percent of respondents around the world say they look for opportunities at work to develop new skills.

There's also another facet at play today. The twenty-first century worker also desires *career security*. Today's workers are acutely aware that they must continually grow to remain marketable, building skills and knowledge they can apply in their current companies or take with them if they leave or are let go. This sort of individual growth is very different and more complex than in the past and increasingly requires workers to have both a global and local business perspective; be both a right- and left-brain thinker; and exhibit a mix of technical and managerial skills. In pursuit of career security, employees embrace learning opportunities that can touch on all of these areas, whether the new skills will lead to an immediate promotion or not.

Most employers can't guarantee job security, but they can deliver career security as a by-product of a learning culture and, in turn, produce more skilled and engaged employees. While it may seem counterintuitive to equip workers with skills that could make them more marketable to the competition, it's important to remember that most people feel more connected and committed to employers that are, in turn, committed to helping them grow.

At North Shore–LIJ, Emily Kao began her career as a pharmacist and is now an associate executive director overseeing clinical services. Kao has turned down several job offers because she says North Shore–LIJ exceeds what competitors provide when it comes to career development. "It shows their commitment to empower employees. They are saying, 'Yes, we will help you because it will help us,'" says Kao, who has been promoted five times in her twenty-three years with North Shore–LIJ. "From a benefit perspective, it's extraordinary. After all, I'm still learning."

Kao's sentiment is at the heart of the most engaging cultures. The resulting increase in employee retention and the reduction in employee turnover cost more than offset the incremental investments companies make in training and development.

Grow from the Top

Leaders must set the agenda and set the example. They need to demonstrate a personal belief in the power of intellectual challenge and natural curiosity to unleash human potential. More practically, C-level executives need to visibly sponsor company-wide learning efforts. When the CEO truly thinks individual growth—including his or her own—will benefit the greater organization, managers at all levels will mirror that commitment.

Foster "Students of Wisdom" at Every Level

Campbell Soup Company CEO Doug Conant describes himself as a perennial "student of wisdom." Today, the thirty-two-year food industry veteran routinely scours leadership articles for insight into how he might "be just a little bit better tomorrow than I am today"; hundreds of management and leadership books fill his office shelves. The extensive collection speaks volumes to everyone who enters Conant's office: here works a chief executive who values learning as much as, if not more than, anyone else.

Real support from top executives in supporting learning initiatives usually begins with senior leaders who truly believe that they, too, have room to grow and to improve. A leader who is not curious, and who is not motivated to learn, doesn't inspire others to do so. Ask yourself if you are continuing to grow, if you are able to share and discuss new ideas or knowledge, and whether you share newly acquired perspectives and skills with others.

Engaged and engaging senior leaders actively champion their own growth. This sends a powerful signal to the workforce. It also forces senior executives to take action in areas they might otherwise have given limited time and attention, or ignored. At the highest levels of management, growth via exposure to people and ideas outside the company is key. And once new knowledge is acquired, senior leaders need to make a point to share it with their peers and direct reports.

Engaging leaders also encourage growth in others. They understand that their senior teams, no matter what their pedigrees and track records, still have the capacity and desire to grow personally and professionally.

At REI, CEO Sally Jewell is obsessed with growing her executive team: "All the time I think, 'What do I owe the people who work for me . . . how can I develop them as leaders?' My legacy will not be what I do while I am here, but how well I prepared them and the people under them to take over."

Note her dual sentiment: Jewell feels she "owes" something to both her employees and the company. Indeed, engaging leaders support learning for the good of the individual worker as well as for the good of the organization. Better yet, Jewell's attitude has filtered through the ranks. Each month at REI's headquarters and distribution center in Kent, Washington, the training and development team hands out copies of business-related and other books to each department. The only instruction: voluntarily sign up to read one and then share it with a colleague. The aptly named Pass It Forward reading program makes it easy—and cost-free— for employees to absorb ideas in classic business tomes, as well as the latest bestsellers. Pass It Forward titles have ranged from Dale Carnegie's *How to Win Friends and Influence People* to more recent approaches to conflict management. At REI, growth begins with the CEO and continues to spread organically throughout the organization.

Senior leaders are also able to foster learning at every level by holding managers accountable for developing and executing personal development plans for themselves and their direct reports. When employee development is not tied into the criteria determining managers' pay and promotions, it often gets ignored or pushed to the bottom of a manager's priority list. Typically, organizations measure how well a manager has met this goal by monitoring the number of their direct reports who have advanced or who are deemed promotable, as well as through 360-degree feedback.

Not all managers have the natural skills to foster an environment of continuous learning and development. That's why it's critical for companies to coach managers on this important aspect of their jobs. We'll discuss the notion of teaching managers to manage later in the chapter, but the key point here is that senior leaders, including the CEO, must *build clear and defined accountability for learning and growth*. That's essential to making sure that manager training is taken seriously, and that managers feel empowered to take ownership of their own growth as well as that of the people they supervise. Ultimately, leaders' behaviors and expectations trickle down and determine whether continuous learning thrives or dies.

A GRAND GESTURE

There must be tangible evidence—a grand gesture—that communicates the CEO's passion for ongoing employee growth. It's impossible for a CEO to look every employee in the eye to drive home his or her commitment, but grand gestures in the form of visible and far-reaching behaviors, programs, or policies become a company-wide symbol of the chief's dedication. Grand gestures are more than a bullet in a PowerPoint presentation of company values; they are defined by their symbolic potential to leave an emotional impression on every worker, and they lead to action. Even seemingly small acts that are done consistently—such as a CEO who shakes every new employee's hand—create a sort of lore that contributes to shaping culture.

At North Shore–LIJ, CEO Dowling made his first grand gesture within weeks of taking over. He created a new executive position, Chief Learning Officer, to which he appointed Dr. Kathleen Gallo, a former emergency room nurse with a PhD in business and nursing. Gallo reports directly to Dowling and not only oversees corporate human resources, but an $11 million university she created, North Shore–LIJ's Center for Learning and Innovation (CLI). Gallo also created the Patient Safety Institute, where nurses and doctors learn by simulating patient care. In 2007, more than 15,000 employees participated in North Shore–LIJ's course offerings, up from 3,000 in 2004.

Dowling and Gallo based the CLI on leading education programs at organizations outside the health care industry, like those at GE and Harvard University. Indeed, five years ago, the CLI was one of the health care industry's only corporate-style universities; today it's the largest, as many more hospitals have imitated North Shore's example. With its mix of management, operational, and clinical courses, Dowling says the CLI is "the primary conduit through which we transmit new ideas and involve the employees in helping us come up with solutions to deliver better health care." He deems participation in CLI programs so critical that employee attendance is tracked and figured into their managers' performance reviews. In fact, workers are encouraged to call Dowling or Gallo directly if a manager hinders their efforts to attend CLI courses.

Many engaging companies have corporate universities similar to North Shore–LIJ's CLI, and there are multiple benefits to venues dedicated to employee education—whether virtual or brick-and-mortar. Assuming the venue offers truly relevant courses to business as well as individual growth, employees interpret such efforts as important symbols of their employer's commitment to professional development. Often, these facilities also provide an opportunity to learn in a different site, far from busy offices, the lure of e-mail, and the pressure of ringing phones. Corporate universities also allow employees from different locations to come together, share ideas, and establish collaborative relationships that will last long after courses end.

Grand gestures can take other forms. At North Shore–LIJ, the emphasis on education extends beyond its own interests to the greater health care industry. Under Dowling, North Shore–LIJ is one of only six organizational supporters of Forces of Change, an ongoing, annual seminar focused on improving the nation's health care system and taught through the Harvard University School of Public Health. Dowling makes the time to attend the session each year to teach leadership in the health care industry.

How leaders such as Dowling spend their time also connotes priorities, especially since employees will take note. Sometimes the simple act of "showing up" can leave a deep impression. Every Monday at 7:30 a.m., for example, Dowling speaks for ninety minutes with newly hired employees—from hospital administrators to allied health professionals—who assemble at the CLI for orientation. Afterward, new employees often introduce themselves to Dowling. It's not uncommon for new hires to tell him that in all their years spent employed by other hospitals they never met the

CEO. Dowling and members of his executive team also teach employee classes at the CLI. North Shore–LIJ's chief financial officer is the dean of finance, and Dowling himself leads management instruction.

Incorporating executives into the teaching process is becoming a more common practice. At MGM Grand, President Gamal Aziz teaches the opening and closing courses for senior leaders at the company's $20 million corporate university. Aziz wants to be "the first and last person employees see" during their formal training. MGM Grand University provides some 280,000 annual hours of employee training, which has helped to promote thousands of workers as well as rank MGM Grand as high as number twenty-eight on the prestigious list of *Training Magazine*'s Top 125 corporate universities. Indeed, MGM Grand University is itself another example of the potency of grand gestures.

Create a Safe Place to Fail and Learn

Failure and mistakes are inherent, necessary pieces of the learning and development process. A child who touches a hot oven quickly learns not to do it again. Even world-class athlete and basketball legend Michael Jordan once declared in a Gatorade commercial that he missed more than 9,000 shots, lost almost 300 games, and missed 26 game-winning baskets. Said Jordan, "I've failed over and over and over again in my life. That is why I succeed."

Given that failure is inevitable in life, in school, and in sports, should it be less tolerated in the workplace? To be sure, failure's consequences can be far-reaching in business, but its learning potential must be leveraged. Just because people are experts in their particular field and are paid to deliver results does not mean they will succeed at every turn. Leaders who tolerate only perfection set themselves and others up for failure and miss opportunities for future success because many mistakes are invaluable learning experiences. Sometimes, the worst mistakes are the ones that enable people—and organizations—to make great leaps in development.

Google is routinely held up as a company that thrives, in part, because it allows employees to fail without severe repercussions. In an interview with National Public Media, *Fortune* writer Adam Lashinsky discussed his article about Google and recalled a senior executive who ran Google's automated advertising systems. The woman had made a multimillion-dollar mistake, and once she recognized her error, she ran across Google's campus and told Google cofounder Larry Page. His reaction, according to Lashinsky, illustrates how much Page valued mistakes as a path to success: "Yeah, we shouldn't have done that. We'll know better next time. But, oh, by the way, it's good that you made this mistake. I'm glad," he told her, "because we need to be the kind of company that is willing to make mistakes. Because if we're not making mistakes, then we're not taking risks. And if we're not taking risks, we won't get to the next level."

If leaders do not recognize mistakes as an inevitable cost of learning, people will become paralyzed by a fear of failure, and that fear thwarts their ability to try anything new. By the same token, leaders should not consider themselves immune from mistakes or assume they can prevent mistakes at every turn. While the CEO must often take the fall for headline-making blunders—recall when JetBlue Airway's founder David Neeleman lost his job after a winter storm in 2007 kept hundreds of furious passengers trapped on JetBlue planes for hours—the belief in a superhero CEO is evaporating. Workers are letting go of the old-school notion that the one person in charge possesses all the answers. We increasingly want and admire evidence of humanity, even humility, in our leaders.

At McKesson, CEO John Hammergren has led the company to achieve impressive financial results since 2000. Yet, when Hammergren is a guest lecturer for McKesson's advanced management courses for top executives, he uses the story of his own career path to illustrate the value—and inevitability—of ongoing learning. "I make no secret of the fact that I am a better CEO today than the day I landed the job. I also talk about my evolution in thinking as a manager, from managing front-line hourly workers to managing executive officers, and how I have had to learn and adapt my style. I try to encourage learning by using my own experience as an example. No one is born as a senior vice president," says Hammergren.

Leaders who acknowledge their own learning curves give employees permission to ask their own questions in an effort to prevent missteps. They don't treat employees who ask for assistance as ignorant. Obvious as it may be, the following truth bears repeating in many organizations: it takes a smart person to know what she does not know, and a confident person to admit as much to herself and others. Engaging managers honor this trait. Says North Shore–LIJ President Dowling: "It's okay to take risks and make mistakes. A person who never makes a mistake never does a damn thing. He never gets up; he stays in bed all day."

Grow with Purpose

Engaging organizations pursue *purposeful* growth opportunities. From an organizational standpoint, they design structured or formal experiences that not only challenge employees and build their skills, but support broad business strategies as well. No company can afford to let people learn just what they want at the company's expense. Effective education must reflect both the organization's and employees' needs to deliver a measurable ROI for both parties.

ALIGN LEARNING WITH BUSINESS GOALS

Learning and development—and, in a broader context, all engagement efforts—must reflect the organization's business goals and strategy.

At the highest level, organizations pursue a handful of strategies to distinguish themselves from the competition. As we discussed in chapter 1, while most companies combine various strategic elements to approach the marketplace uniquely, one line of attack tends to predominate. Novartis, for example, emphasizes new product innovation. Retailer REI aspires to deliver a superb customer experience.

North Shore–LIJ's goal of becoming a world-class health care provider involves more than curing illness and conducting groundbreaking research. A world-class hospital ensures that patients are treated with the same sense of efficiency and respect that consumers have come to expect from, say, a retailer or a restaurant. Anyone who has gone to an emergency room and waited hours to be admitted knows how frustrated he or she feels after the experience, even if the outcome was good. What do people do with that frustration? They complain to friends and family about their lousy hospital visit, and as a result those people may choose to go elsewhere next time they have a choice. Such word-of-mouth marketing chips away at a health care facility's reputation, its business, and employee morale.

Engaging leaders such as North Shore–LIJ's Dowling understand the link between customer service and engagement. "If I walk into a restaurant and have a pissed-off waiter, I am not going to be happy with the treatment I receive," he says. Extrapolate his point to health care: what pregnant woman wants an unmotivated physician or a dissatisfied nurse at her side as she goes through the poignant, and often scary, life experience of delivering her first baby into the world? This type of realization is consistently taking root at all levels of the North Shore–LIJ workforce thanks to a learning and development curriculum that gears education toward providing a better patient experience.

It's easy for a company to say it links employee learning to its business strategy. It's much more difficult to do. But with a clear understanding of a company's strategic model—and the employee actions that affect outcomes like high customer satisfaction, revenue, and profitability—it is possible to define behaviors, skills, and information that employees in different roles must have to deliver the desired results.

Using an approach we call Value Driver Analysis, an organization can, first, define and translate its business priorities into specific worker behaviors that drive those goals and, second, use that translation to inform how it designs learning and development opportunities. Value Driver Analysis breaks down each financial measure to its basic building blocks and identifies the key actions that influence the foundational measures. We use Value Driver Analysis to help companies ensure close alignment between how they make money and the specific policies and programs needed to ensure that employees are focused on the right things to deliver strong financial results.

To vastly oversimplify, a Value Driver Analysis might reveal that a hotel chain's profits are heavily dependent on repeat business and that the principal reasons it draws repeat customers is the combination of convenient locations and a broad set of business services. That knowledge is essential for managers to make the right decisions about where to expand and how to design and service the hotels. For a slightly more detailed description of this critical tool, see Exhibit E: Value Driver Analysis at Work.

In identifying the precise components of financial value in a business, it also becomes clearer which roles contribute most to the company. Based on the outcome of the Value Driver Analysis, we can evaluate which jobs broadly fit into the four job categories identified in chapter 2 (see page 68). This assessment can help your organization isolate what jobs drive value and where training investments are most likely to pay off. For instance, because strategic jobs directly affect the company's main strategy, they must consistently be developed and nurtured and should receive a significant share of training dollars and time. Core jobs, by contrast, affect company strategy less directly and thus typically do not call for as great an investment of either money or time.

To examine this more specifically, let's use an airline as an example. Say the airline's primary strategy is to deliver a superior passenger experience to its most frequent and high-margin fliers (primarily business travelers) to gain their loyalty and travel dollars. Among the airline's *strategic* employees are those who directly interact with the target customers, including first- and business-class flight attendants, and select call-center service representatives. Mechanics hold *core* jobs because they are necessary to keep the airline running, but after meeting a certain technical threshold, they don't affect the high-margin passengers' experience. Finally, catering staff for coach meals may be deemed a *support* role and perhaps can be outsourced to a moderately priced catering company.

Exhibit E: Value Driver Analysis at Work

Value Driver Analysis can be most easily understood by way of example. Below are two illustrations from an actual retail grocery outlet. The first part of this analysis shows how the company makes money and what aspects of store operations are most critical to its customer-profit chain. The second part focuses on the specific attributes of the stores and the aspects under employees' control that, in turn, affect customer buying patterns and, ultimately, profitability.

Starting with our first illustration and working from right to left, we see that the company's key financial metric, operating profit, is defined by gross profit offset by operating expenses (sales, general and administration, or SG&A), and depreciation and amortization. Next, we see what drives gross profit, which is total sales minus the cost of goods sold (COGS) and an element called "shrink," which is the loss of inventory due to things like theft and damage.

Taking another step backward, we can then define the types of product sales that make up gross sales and, in yet another step backward, the store operations and customer experience that impact customers' loyalty and buying habits. Note, for instance, that these include things over which employees can have a relatively high degree of control, including their knowledge, friendliness, and helpfulness, as well as the quality of the produce and meats, the nature of specials and sales, and so on.

Not all these elements have the same impact on sales, and the exercise helps identify the actual versus perceived value of each. A further statistical analysis may reveal that small improvements in checkout time (adding another checker during the store's busiest hours, for example) may improve sales just as much or more than larger and more costly changes, such as adding organic fruits and vegetables. With the benefit of these insights, senior managers may see that speed is more profitable than product selection and thus opt to train more company personnel in

Value Driver Analysis at Work
(continued)

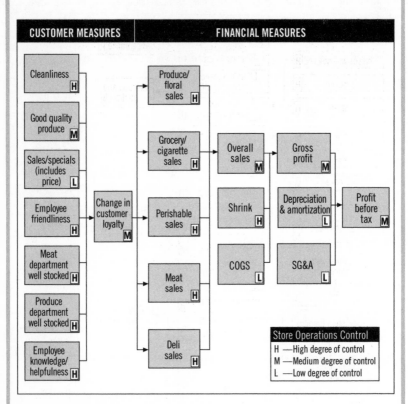

customer service and checkout than, say, building out inventory and sourcing new merchandise.

Armed with this kind of information, any organization or business unit has an empirical basis for determining and prioritizing those capabilities that are most beneficial to build (and, conversely, which can be minimized or eliminated). Training and development decisions will then reflect the mission-critical jobs and behaviors that the Value Driver Analysis has revealed.

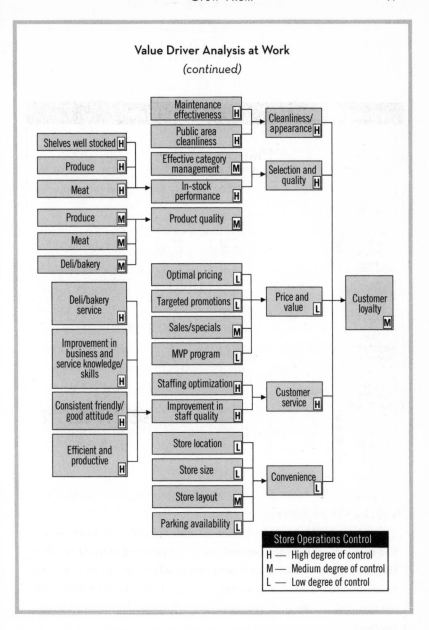

Value Driver Analysis at Work
(continued)

This view of roles relative to strategy and financial success doesn't mean nonstrategic employees should not receive training or should be excluded from development programs. Rather, it helps the organization focus its most significant and potentially costliest development activities in the manner that will yield the best return on that investment. For our airline, that means maintaining exceptional service capabilities of call-center representatives and flight attendants because their positions have the greatest potential to garner significant customer loyalty and, thus, improved financial performance.

Once strategic jobs are identified, an organization must then determine the primary competencies—that is, specific skills, abilities, and knowledge—that those individual jobholders need to have to successfully execute the business strategy. A Value Driver Analysis should identify the most important competencies. While some of these are general competencies, many will be unique to an organization and have the potential to significantly differentiate a company from competitors. In the case of our airline, every business traveler's experience—from making a reservation to disembarking the plane—must be as comfortable and problem-free as possible.

The airline's competencies for the flight attendants and call-center representatives would likely include excellent communication skills and effective conflict-resolution abilities, among others. In order for our airline to provide the desired customer experience on the phone, for instance, a call-center operator must understand and clearly speak a customer's native language and be enthusiastic or empathetic when appropriate. Relevant training courses for call-center representatives might include language classes and how to read verbal cues for stress and anger. Other learning activities might include "shadowing" colleagues on customer calls to learn additional nuances and jargon and to observe appropriate responses to caller comments. The result is an ability to seamlessly interact with a high-margin customer.

Alternatively, for flight attendants to provide the desired customer experience, they must be able to calmly pacify frustrated fliers, even the most demanding and intimidating ones. Appropriate training might therefore include role-playing a sales executive sitting in seat 2B whose delayed flight made him lose a lucrative account. By putting herself in the shoes of the airline's most valued customers, the attendant will learn to be more empathetic and thus remain calm and pleasant the next time a passenger blames her for a snowstorm. In turn, the passenger will feel less angry by the time his plane lands and not resolve to take his business elsewhere. The airline example demonstrates how, by drilling down from a macro to a micro level, a company can link its business strategy to specific employee competencies and behavior, and focus its training on ensuring key employees do the right things in the right ways.

Such targeted training is particularly important for the growing number of companies and industries competing for diminishing talent pools. Demographic realities mean it is not always possible to "buy" required competencies on the street—and certainly not at the level required to remain competitive. A 2006 study by Manpower shows that many companies are already having trouble filling jobs in sales, engineering, and accounting—and these gaps are expected to grow. Leading organizations need to begin building skills in these areas proactively, before they're forced to do so and have less of a chance to get a jump start on their competitors. That typically means hiring more people at an entry level and building clear career paths with well-defined training and development plans for these individuals.

Ultimately, helping people develop the right competencies over the course of their careers is the most effective way of ensuring a company can successfully differentiate its products and services, and the kind of experience it provides its customers.

Combine Learning with Real-World Problem Solving

One of the most purposeful and powerful ways to teach is to have employees solve specific problems that plague the organization, either in a classroom setting or on the job. Such experiential learning can take many forms: a six-month course; a supervisor who encourages a direct report to come up with a creative solution for a chronic business problem; even internal competitions among employees. In every case, employees learn through a process of discovery and application; many times, the results can immediately support the business.

At North Shore–LIJ, real-world improvement projects are part of CLI education, and since 2001, employees have tackled more than 260 such projects. For example, after completing a ten-course management program through CLI, employees are assigned a so-called Capstone project to which they apply newly acquired knowledge to improve a process in a specific area of the hospital system. Larger, cross-departmental procedures that need improvement are assigned to employees who take CLI courses in Six Sigma and LEAN—standardized process improvement methodologies designed to reduce mistakes and increase efficiency.

In 2005, a group of employees—including a radiology technician, a physician, a hospital transporter, a physician's assistant, and a secretary—had four days to reduce the twenty-one-hour average turnaround time it took for computer tomography (CAT scan) results to become available at one of North Shore–LIJ's hospitals. First, the CLI "students" were taught LEAN techniques to analyze the entire CAT scan process, from the moment a doctor orders the test to the moment a patient completes the procedure. Eventually, they identified erroneous assumptions that affected the timing of scheduled appointments. The group's recommendations not only decreased the average CAT scan turnaround to eleven hours, but increased the number of CAT scans the department could schedule in a day, from forty-five to fifty-two, without increasing staff or purchasing more equipment. This helped increase patient satisfaction, which in turn increased employee engagement. Most impressive, the changes increased revenue because the department was able to schedule more outpatient procedures, which are more lucrative than in-patient CAT scans.

At EMC, where innovation is the technology behemoth's lifeblood (recall that its current revenue stream comes almost entirely from products and services introduced in the last two years), experiential learning spurs technological creativity, while simultaneously keeping EMC's high-performing workforce challenged. Let's look at this through the lens of one employee, forty-two-year-old software engineer Stephen Todd, whose job is to create new IT storage products. Todd, who joined EMC when it acquired his company in 1999, is the founder of a major product that, since hitting the market in the early 1990s, has shipped more than 250,000 units. Here's how Todd describes EMC's strengths:

> I feel like a kid in a candy store here. What I want is the ability to be creative, and of the many companies I've heard of, EMC challenges employees the most. It sets the bar very high. The expectation from senior management is, "Yes, I want you to be creative but this is not an academic environment. It's not homework. We need it quickly and we need it to satisfy a certain market." . . . There are so many opportunities to build

interesting products, and that's the reason I like work the most.

Todd has filed more than 140 technology-based patents as part of an EMC-sponsored program that awards a bonus to any employee who files a patent with the U.S. Patent and Trademark Office. Todd also finished his advanced degree while working full-time, and EMC helped him identify a master's thesis that would benefit the company and satisfy his degree. His paper, about industry standards for a specific type of storage technology, helped maintain EMC's position as an industry leader in the marketplace, while providing practical solutions. Says Todd, "I did not just work on a thesis that gave me a degree, but I produced something highly relevant."

Todd also stretches his mind by participating in real-world problem-solving contests, including a company-wide Innovation Conference that allows employees to submit improvement ideas for any area of the organization, from products to process control. On a smaller scale, individual EMC project teams frequently hold online contests, inviting colleagues to submit solutions to solve specific customer dilemmas. Todd recently submitted an idea to one client team that needed help figuring out the best way to migrate customer data from one storage product to another. The winner would get $5,000. "The money is nice, but the process of putting it all together is the fun part," says Todd. "These contests take you out of your comfort zone. I have a day-to-day job that I know how to do very well. To have my company say, 'Hey, take a break to do something that is fun but still benefits the company,' that's refreshing."

Other real-world educational approaches, at EMC and other organizations, include:

- Sending people on the road to visit other company facilities. When employees tour a warehouse, store, or an office in a different part of the country or in another part of the world, it exposes them to new ways of doing business that they will inevitably share with colleagues back "home."

- Facilitating opportunities for employees to interact with customers at noncritical junctures. As part of its formal training, EMC has emerging leaders meet with its top clients for face-to-face briefings and question-and-answer sessions. They leave with a better understanding of the marketplace as well as client needs and expectations. Indeed, just such a meeting led to the creation of one of EMC's most successful products.

- Letting employees "fill the void," or step up, when workers above them are away from the organization for any period of time. When people take a leave of absence or are on vacation, they delegate day-to-day responsibilities—not major decisions—to someone else. Literally, this means letting an employee walk in the boss's shoes or sit in her chair for a set period of time. Exposing workers firsthand to the types of daily challenges they may one day face is an incredible experience that will help them understand the skills and knowledge they need.

- Establishing job rotation programs. EMC moves employees around early in their careers to ensure a well-rounded education. Says EMC head of HR Jack Mollen, "If you don't have a variety of functional experiences, it's going to be impossible to be a leader at EMC. And we want to develop as many P&L leaders as we can. If people are going to have the ability to run a product business, they need experience in at least two of three areas: marketing, sales, and engineering."

Upon completing several rotations, employees are placed in an area that best suits their skills and interests.

Here are a few important guidelines for choosing real-world, experiential learning projects. Such assignments should be strategic, but not urgent. While the outcome should impact the company, it should not be a fix so dramatic that the shareholders or the board of directors are already awaiting the answer. And don't put learning teams on a crisis. Some of the most appropriate experiential projects focus on long-term strategies, challenging employees to look out five or more years and predict how the organization might respond to potential trends or changing market conditions. In many cases, their solutions may become tomorrow's revenue source.

Personalize Growth

To engage employees, personalize formal and informal growth opportunities. It's well documented that people learn in a variety of ways. Some need to *see* content; others need to *experience* it. Still others learn best by reading. Yet, everyone benefits from repetition and reinforcement. An employee's training should reflect her role and potential future roles at the company, an accurate assessment of her strengths and weaknesses, as well as her ambition, interests, learning style, and experience. When employers challenge their people and develop their careers in ways that resonate with them on a personal level, increased engagement usually follows.

Customize Learning Experiences with Variety

Every individual has a predisposition to learn in a certain way. Different learning styles are based on a number of factors, including how people receive and discern information, how they process that information, how they make decisions, and how they act. Some people are visual learners, others more auditory. Some learn by active participation, others by observation. Culture and past experience color how individuals absorb and retain new material. An individual's interests and needs at various ages and stages of their career are also factors in the best developmental experience. For example, a new college graduate may be eager to work abroad, while a Baby Boomer may be more interested in gaining global experience by collaborating with a multicultural team in his home country. While few if any organizations have the resources to customize education for each employee, a flexible program with a variety of components will enable a vast majority of workers to absorb, retain, and apply what they learn.

There is no tactical silver bullet that dictates, for instance, that all twenty-somethings learn best online, or that three-day conferences are a waste of time and money. From our *Global Workforce Study*, though, we do know that while workers gravitate to a variety of learning experiences, they prefer real-world learning: 82 percent of our global respondents identified on-the-job training as the type of professional development most important to them. Other training avenues received more mixed views from respondents in terms of preference:

- 50 percent preferred classroom training.
- 37 percent preferred shadowing.
- 34 percent preferred apprenticeships.
- 28 percent preferred conferences.
- 27 percent preferred simulation.
- 27 percent preferred e-training.

While employees clearly lean toward classroom education over e-training, that does not mean organizations should eliminate computer-based learning programs. We've just stepped into this new venue in the last several years, and its effectiveness across generations is still evolving. Every learning venue—from e-learning to corporate universities to partnerships with local colleges and tuition reimbursement programs—has value, and the most engaging organizations provide a mix of teaching mechanisms. C-level executives and HR professionals have the power to create and budget for a variety of learning experiences, as well as centralize ongoing learning initiatives for consistency throughout the organization.

Here's an example. MGM Grand has, as you would imagine, an immense culinary operation, for both guests and its nearly 10,000 employees. Not only do chefs prepare daily meals, but they research tomorrow's innovative menu items. To keep its chefs on the cutting edge of cuisine, MGM Grand provides creative opportunities for them to grow their cooking skills. Johannes Diele, the assistant vice president of catering, oversees MGM Grand's convention kitchens, enormous facilities that prepare 650,000 dinners annually for the hotel's convention guests. Every week, as part of his learning initiatives, Diele asks a different employee to research a food-related topic of his or her choice and present the information to colleagues. The peer-to-peer lessons inspire new menu ideas, as well as enhanced communication skills. Another boss in MGM Grand's culinary division arranges for chefs to meet with and shadow world-renowned chefs, a relationship these individuals could never initiate on their own but value forever.

MGM Grand also hosts what it calls a Culinary Challenge, a cook-off of sorts that pits chefs from the hotel's various kitchens against each other. Each chef is given the same ingredients and limited time to prepare a dish that is judged by colleagues. The contest has taken on a cult status at MGM Grand; competition is friendly, but chefs take it seriously and treat it as a chance to sharpen as well as display their talent in front of colleagues and management.

What seems like fun and games at MGM Grand is actually a serious, successful effort to build workers both purposefully and personally from within. The chefs at the finest MGM Grand restaurants—Nobhill, Craftsteak, L'Atelier, and Seablue—consider themselves not just cooks at a casino, but experts in the culinary arts. While these chefs could work at hundreds of Las Vegas dining establishments, they choose MGM Grand in part because the organization is serious about helping them perfect their craft. In turn, when MGM Grand opens new restaurants or has positions open at its venues, it's able to staff from within, tapping existing talent and employees who already fit into its culture.

The secret ingredient is to offer workers a menu of learning options. When given a choice, employees will gravitate to the methods that best suit their style.

Personalize Growth for High-Potentials

The desire to grow may be greatest for high-performing and highly ambitious employees. These are also the people your organization needs most. When it comes to development, this population de-mands special attention. Basically, high-potentials believe they must "grow or go." In other words, if a top performer does not believe her company is enhancing her skills, she'll find an employer that will. It's imperative to create unique growth opportunities targeting this ambitious group, not only to build future leaders, but to engage and retain them today. The key, of course, is to mesh the individual's needs with those of the business.

At MGM Grand, President Gamal Aziz credits educational

programs geared at high-achievers with creating bench strength the
company never had before. His philosophy mirrors programs we
see in other engaging cultures: "Education here is a reward, not a
punishment. Development is a source of pride, and we select the
best to attend our university. People who get in know they are there
because they are the best." While MGM Grand University offers
dozens of individual classes for which any employee may sign up—
from computer instruction to Spanish—there are four exclusive,
invitation-only programs.

For one program, twenty senior executives are invited annually to
attend MGM Grand's Leadership Institute, twenty-four weeks of
practical education that prepares participants for higher positions.
College professors, consultants, topical experts, authors, and MGM
Grand's own executives, including Aziz and MGM Mirage chairman Terry Lanni, teach classes. The executives explain, for instance,
how Wall Street evaluates public companies; how to understand
what's discussed during quarterly conference calls between MGM
Mirage executives and industry analysts; even how to read the *Wall
Street Journal*. There are lessons in government regulation, such
as how legislation can affect the gaming industry and why the
organization supports specific candidates and participates in various
lobbying efforts. In essence, the Leadership Institute teaches basic
business literacy to a select group. In lieu of tests, employees are
graded on their level of participation. Since 2002, 53 percent of
Leadership Institute graduates have received promotions, a level
with which Aziz is quite pleased.

The invitation-only approach to learning should not be reserved
for the executive set. That's why MGM Grand also offers REACH!,
an intense six-month program that teaches basic supervisory skills
to hourly workers who want to advance into management. Eighty
salaried workers are selected from more than 200 applicants and

treated like management during their REACH! training. Each week, REACH! participants attend a three-hour class focused on business basics such as public speaking, writing, and conflict management. Classes include guest speakers, case studies, even role-playing. REACH! students are also assigned managers in their department who help with homework assignments and provide a hands-on management perspective. Another program for aspiring managers allows employees to sit in on management-level meetings held throughout the company. That exposure is a big deal for ambitious salaried employees like forty-one-year-old Michael Solas, who works in MGM Grand's payroll department:

> Management meetings are not mandatory, but I've been to all except one since I've been allowed to go. They talk about financial updates regarding quarterly results, which I find very interesting. They go over any property changes regarding restaurants . . . I get to hear Gamal speak at the beginning and the end, which I find enlightening . . . I write down everything.

More than 60 percent of the REACH! graduates have been promoted at MGM Grand since the program launched in 2003.

Another effective approach is to give high-potentials the freedom to grow themselves. This approach works well with the most enthusiastic, curious workers who actively look for problems to solve and challenge themselves. When you give these go-getters opportunities rather than orders, they rise to the occasion and push themselves beyond their limits, even beyond their main job responsibilities.

This approach can be difficult for some managers because it requires them to give up a degree of control. North Shore–LIJ's

Dowling explains, "A lot of employees want to find a better way to do things, but managers act like wet blankets and stifle innovation because they are so insecure about letting other people's ideas blossom. They think management is about control, but it is possible to increase your control by giving it up. The more people push the envelope, the more everyone will improve." While some workers thrive on direction, others are more likely to take on challenging situations if they feel the opportunity is being offered to them, not foisted on them. They see inherent value in the freedom to choose their own path.

At Campbell, for example, Amanda Tolino is a twenty-five-year-old communications specialist for the company's community relations programs. Tolino says her friends at other companies—other Millennials—often complain to each other about their boring jobs and terrible bosses, but she is smitten with Campbell and intent on staying as long as she can. And Campbell wants to keep her. In less than a year, Tolino's initiatives have made quite an impact. She created a system to track the volunteer work Campbell employees do each year, a metric never measured in the past. She established relationships with other employees at Campbell's warehouses and company store, and encouraged them to ship her overstocked and aging products so she could fulfill some $15,000 worth of annual donation requests from employees and local community groups. And, Tolino recruited eighty Campbell employees to read weekly to elementary schoolchildren severely behind in their reading skills.

No one told Tolino to do any of these tasks, but thanks to a boss who gave Tolino freedom to accomplish business goals, Campbell reaps the benefits of her initiative. The community relations department saves thousands of dollars annually by *not* purchasing products for external donations because the food is "donated" by other Campbell divisions that would have probably thrown away the unused products. As for the schoolchildren, their reading skills surged more than one grade level in just sixteen reading sessions, an accomplishment that inspires pride among the employee volunteers and bodes well for Campbell's local reputation as a corporate citizen.

This is what Tolino has done for Campbell after just a year on the job. Imagine what her go-getter attitude will do for the company in five or more years. This, of course, begs the question: What's Campbell doing for Tolino to keep her so engaged? The biggest single thing that keeps her happy, she says, is "the opportunity for career development and growth." She also credits her boss for always listening to her ideas and giving her the freedom to explore them. "Let me give you another example," she volunteered, and explained how she is creating an internal employee network of other Campbell twenty-somethings who will get together, share ideas, and eventually talk to other generations employed at Campbell about what it takes to motivate her generation of workers. "I think it will bring great business value and help Campbell remain on the cutting edge." says Tolino. "As for me, I'm given the opportunity to lead a project that has nothing to do with my job, but that will give me feedback from executives whom ordinarily I would not interact with, and gain skills I can use in any job I hold here . . ."

Tolino, like high-potential employees at other organizations, came to her job hardwired to grow. Because she was given the flexibility to pursue projects that were of greatest interest to her, she essentially personalized her own on-the-job learning agenda. The freedom in and of itself is perhaps the most engaging gift that Campbell could give a high-potential like Tolino, and we suspect that her frustrated friends at other companies would say they envy her opportunity.

OFFER TRANSPARENT, STRATEGIC, AND LATERAL CAREER PATHS

Today's workers require, indeed demand, the ability to visualize potential career paths at their current organization. But these talent management and career development efforts must blend strategic business goals with an individual's interests.

Engaging organizations and engaging bosses don't just ask a worker how she wants to grow and where she wants to go in her career. They proactively share information about a variety of roles the organization will need to fill in the years ahead, as well as what the worker can do to be considered for various positions given her aptitude. The individual, in turn, should have an opportunity to choose her path given the information her employer provided, as well as her ambitions, interests, and values.

This "career pathing" process enables organizations to develop and deploy talent purposefully as well as personally. Increasingly, organizations manage career pathing via an integrated set of career ladders (see Exhibit F on page 108) for each of the various business functions, such as production, management, marketing, or human resources. When these ladders are integrated, they form a jungle gym of sorts that clarify the skills, knowledge, and abilities needed at each point. These structures also offer employees a tangible way to visualize a variety of career routes throughout the company. Routes may include moving up vertically, taking lateral steps, or making other nontraditional moves. In this way, career pathing provides a level of transparency and structure that helps employees—especially those in global organizations—see opportunities beyond their local office.

Because career pathing allows for lateral and vertical movements— cross-functional experiences and cross-geography assignments—it not only helps companies view career development more broadly but also ensures that employees are more qualified for future jobs.

And on an emotional level, it creates a sense that the employer respects nontraditional career moves, which employees appreciate even if they never take advantage of them.

From an employee's perspective, career growth is not always equivalent to moving "up" the career ladder. Yet a surprising number of companies today are stuck in an old-school assumption that the only way to advance a career is by being promoted to the next level in a division or department. But for today's workers, career development is not just about *ascending* the ladder. As one chief executive told us, "Not everyone wants to be CEO one day. And that's fine. There's a population of workers who come to work every day and want to be stimulated and energized from eight to four."

Lateral development can take many forms: moving from one location to another in the same job, moving into a new functional area for the company, or moving to a new business unit. Next to experiential growth, learning and development through lateral moves is one of the most effective approaches for organizations to build employees' capabilities. Psychologists have long known that putting adults in unfamiliar situations opens their minds and accelerates their absorption of new knowledge.

Employees who make these moves become more engaged for two reasons. First, their rational connection to the company strengthens as they learn more about the company's operations. Second, their emotional connection increases because of the investment their employer has made in them and the freedom their employer has given them to move.

Lateral development opportunities also engage employees who want to adjust the personal balance in their lives. One example comes from REI, where 79 percent of employees are highly engaged, according to REI's annual internal survey. Seven years ago, one of REI's valued employees, Rachel Ligtenberg, was managing twenty stores, a responsibility that required extensive travel and left little time for her family and community work. When Ligtenberg told her bosses she wanted to "throttle back," they respected her request. She took a new job as general manager of one retail location, REI's high-profile flagship store in Seattle. Ligtenberg admits that

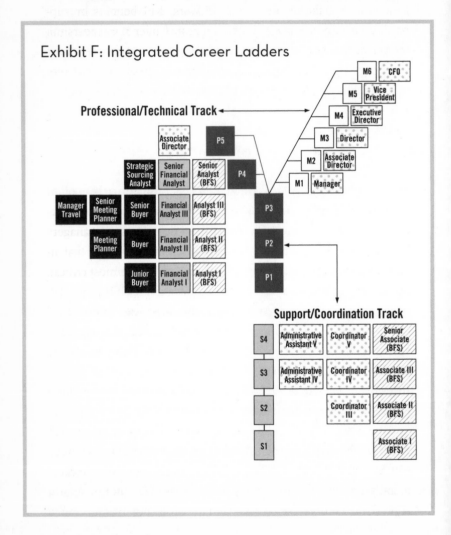

Exhibit F: Integrated Career Ladders

changing from managing multiple stores to one location was an unorthodox career move for someone with the capacity and company-backed confidence to move up. But, more important, Ligtenberg feels REI helped her grow as a person. The new job is still challenging and simultaneously gives her more time for activities outside REI, including family and nonprofit work. REI benefits by supporting Ligtenberg's lateral career request. Under her leadership, the Seattle store's profits grew more than 70 percent between 2001 and 2007. Ligtenberg's career path reinforces the notion that promotions and employee-perceived growth are not always synonymous.

Grow Better Bosses

Much has been researched and written about the importance of an employee's direct boss on his or her job satisfaction and engagement level. While there is no doubt that supervisors or managers have a tremendous influence, the boss is not the only factor that affects employee engagement, and may not even be the most critical. As we saw in previous chapters, the organization itself is as pivotal, if not more so. Without an infrastructure of policies, procedures, and leader-modeled behaviors to back up an individual boss's management style, he is much less powerful in his ability to engage people.

We've discussed how the onus of personalizing the learning experience falls to direct supervisors. Only they are in a position to find out what their individual workers want to learn, to know what the organization needs them to learn, and to know how employees will best absorb the knowledge. Bosses must then help workers identify a career path and build a development plan. But imagine a supervisor who wants to teach and promote her most talented staffers, yet has only her own ingenuity and communication skills to rely on, with no support from classes, books, or permission from senior leaders to try new things. Yes, there are steps she can take to arm her direct reports with new knowledge, but without senior leaders who publicly and enthusiastically champion ongoing learning, and without an arsenal of educational opportunities that simultaneously support business goals and individual employees' interests, a boss can only help her workers grow so much.

In short, it is difficult for bosses to work the system if there is no system to work.

That said, company-wide policies and learning opportunities mean nothing unless direct bosses leverage them. A learning culture cannot be sustained without individual managers who know how to manage, which at the very least means they must know how to talk to and listen to workers. Herein lies a serious problem: *too many of today's managers are ill equipped to communicate with—let alone engage—their direct reports.* Many supervisors were formerly star producers who were promoted into management roles because there was nowhere else for them to go. These folks are all superb creators, but some of them are lousy managers. Engaging companies understand that management in and of itself requires a basic skill set that many supervisors do not possess and must be taught.

Traditionally, teaching supervisors how to "manage" has been relegated to two- or three-day seminars. Yet, it's imperative that companies dispense management advice throughout the year, and in ways that allow supervisors to call upon material and insight at their own pace.

For example, Honeywell improves the management skills of its front-line supervisors via an online, monthly newsletter called *Manager's Journal.* Each issue of the four-page journal addresses basic management techniques—conflict resolution, managing with a global perspective, pay differentiation—in simple, straightforward language. Articles profile Honeywell's employees as examples. One recent column offered alternate ways managers can have productive conversations with direct reports. One plant manager from Ireland said he personally walks the floor of his factory every day because "it is tough for an employee to walk off the plant floor and knock on a supervisor's door with everyone watching." Another manager, whose direct reports are geographically scattered at client sites, calls his staffers on the phone daily, beginning at 6 a.m. "By the first part of the day, I've touched half the team. Mostly, it communicates that I care and that I really want to know what is happening," he said.

These ideas may seem like common sense, but step back and consider just how many workers complain about their bosses—*he doesn't listen . . . she doesn't set clear expectations . . . he isn't helping me get to the next level*—and it becomes obvious that too many supervisors lack basic skills to effectively grow, and thus engage, their own direct reports. Tools such as *Manager's Journal,* or other forums where management advice is readily available, help build the skills of bosses on an ongoing basis.

In Closing: The Growing Worker

North Shore–LIJ's strategic solution to a very specific talent crunch drives home the symbiotic relationship between growing employees with purpose and personalization.

After creating a new neural surgery institute, North Shore–LIJ desperately needed electroencephalogram (EEG) technicians to staff it. Unfortunately, there was a shortage of the specialized practitioners in the New York area. So, North Shore–LIJ created its own supply. First, it partnered with a local university to train existing hospital workers. The school provided North Shore–LIJ with additional instructors and EEG curriculum. To recruit EEG "students," all North Shore–LIJ had to do was ask. "It was like sending out free tickets to a U2 concert!" says Chief Learning Officer Dr. Gallo. "People applied right and left." Upwards of 300 people took the test to qualify for the fifteen-month EEG instruction, which was free to employees. North Shore–LIJ paid the college and held classes at its own Center for Learning and Innovation. People graduated with a certificate that not only qualified them to work in the neural surgery institute, but provided a new career path that would benefit them long after, and if, they ever left the organization.

Willie Walker, a forty-six-year-old, twelve-year veteran of North Shore–LIJ, was an assistant in postsurgery recovery rooms when he first heard about the EEG tech training opportunity:

I always wanted to advance myself, but I own a home and have kids, and most formal education programs are full-time, so it was impossible to go to school and keep my job and benefits. I was in the break-room when I saw a poster inviting employees of good standing to take an admissions test to be trained as an EEG tech. I had always been fascinated with neurology, and the new job would mean an increase in salary and more responsibility. I think everyone should try to take on more responsibility.

I raced to take the test at the CLI and got in. The hospital made it possible for me to keep my job and go to school . . . they brought the teachers to us. I did very well in class and when a position came up, I put together my résumé and recommendations and applied. A few weeks later I got the job, and a few months into the job my boss retired, so I took over her role.

It's been great. To learn, sometimes you just have to get in there and do it, but I have plenty of people to help me if I need it. I call EEG techs from other hospitals all the time if I am not 100 percent sure about what to do in a situation. We all work together here.

This opportunity has taken me to the next level. Now I have a skill that someone can't just walk in off the street and get hired to do. I have built a little bit of security. It's a very serious job, and it puts me on a more professional level, and that makes me proud. We spot things on the machine and patients are helped, so I feel like I'm doing something that makes some type of difference in people's lives. That's the best part of it.

Walker's experience exemplifies the power of a leader-supported, purposeful, and personalized learning and development culture.

By building strategic skills in an existing high-potential employee, North Shore–LIJ staffed a hard-to-fill position internally with someone who became engaged at both the emotional and intellectual level. Thanks to his CEO's belief and investment in ongoing learning programs, Walker had the freedom and opportunity to choose a new career path that not only increased his own career security but also supported the organization's business goals. He flourishes in part from his desire to take on and succeed at new challenges, and also from the support of bosses who wrote his recommendations and the safe culture that continues to cushion his on-the-job learning curve. At an emotional level, Walker's pride in his contribution to patients' health translates every day into how he treats patients, which in turn helps North Shore–LIJ realize a strategic goal: to provide a superior patient-customer experience.

Willie Walker is as engaged as workers get, and North Shore–LIJ is only the better for it.

Inspire Them

Cultivate Pride and Care for Employees' Well-Being

The good things a company does have
a halo effect on employees.
—*Sally Jewell, CEO, REI*

Recreational Equipment, Inc. (REI) Chief Executive Officer Sally Jewell vividly remembers an incident from earlier in her career. It was a minor event, but it informed her current approach toward leadership. One day, another employee complained to Jewell that the president of the company where they both worked "looked right through him" when they passed each other in the corridor. "This was someone who had met with the president multiple times and worked with him for years," recalls Jewell. "The amount of hurt that accrued just stuck with me."

It was, essentially, a lesson in the amount of emotion, positive or negative, that employees tie to their leaders' behavior.

Today, Jewell is keenly aware of the inevitable emotional connection employees develop to their companies' leaders, as well as to their direct bosses. And this emotional connection extends to how employees feel about the companies they work for and how they perceive their jobs and their careers. Since she became COO in

2000 and CEO in 2005—following four years on REI's board of
directors and nineteen years in the banking business—Jewell has
combined operational prowess with personal touch. She may not
know each of REI's 10,000 employees by name, but she takes pains
to say hello if she sees them in the halls of the Kent, Washington,
headquarters or in any one of REI's one hundred stores or
warehouses. It's not unusual for Jewell to stroll into the corporate
café and just sit with employees as they eat lunch or break for coffee.
Explains Jewell, "I just say, 'Can I join you?' and we talk about
whatever they were talking about: the weather, their kids. I do not
intend to talk about work, and I think people just appreciate that I
sit down to chat, and we get to know a little more about each
other."

Personal connection is evident not only in the way Jewell leads,
but in the outdoor gear and clothing retailer's modus operandi.
REI's history is rooted in a passion and respect for outdoor
adventure. In 1938, twenty-three mountain-climbing buddies
founded what today is now the nation's largest consumer cooperative, with more than 3.5 million member-customers who pay a one-
time $20 fee and receive a portion of profits each year, based on a
percentage of their eligible purchases. REI's mission statement—
to inspire, educate, and outfit for a lifetime of outdoor adventure
and stewardship—extends beyond selling gear. Since 1976, REI
has contributed more than $20 million to outdoor recreation clubs
and conservation groups.

Jewell, an engineer by training and former financial industry
executive, does not manage purely with her heart. "There is no
mission without margin," the former banker is fond of saying. She
combines her passion for people and the outdoors with an astute
intelligence for business operations. We share Jewell's view: passion
without profits is pointless. "It's very difficult to make the workplace

a better place if you are suffering a financial crisis. So, you have to run a sound business," she says.

REI is more than sound. In 2007, the co-op had operating income of $106.5 million on revenues of $1.3 billion; it was REI's fifth consecutive record-breaking revenue year. That same year, 79 percent of REI's workforce reported feeling "highly engaged," according to the company's own employee survey.

What does engagement look like at REI?

Engaged store workers dream up and coordinate adventures for customers like canoe outings and hikes that spur interest in the outdoors and, in turn, new product purchases. An engaged salesperson fits a family for hiking boots and also identifies family-friendly trails for them to visit. An engaged store manager makes a point to touch base with every store employee, every day, and regularly talks to managers at nearby stores to compare notes on regional market trends, coordinate inventory, and align marketing activity. Engaged accountants catch paperwork errors, and engaged warehouse workers get products shipped on, if not ahead of, schedule. One highly engaged worker at REI's Anchorage, Alaska, store went the extra fifteen miles (uphill) when he hiked up a mountain to help a customer haul a thirty-pound granite headstone and fifty-pound concrete base for a memorial she wanted to build for her son.

In addition to providing high levels of customer service, engaged employees help increase REI's employee retention rates, decrease recruiting costs, and maintain a robust succession pipeline as well as an enviable reputation. REI's 2007 turnover of hourly, in-store employees was 39 percent. That may sound high relative to most other industries, but in retail it's remarkable compared to an industry average that is close to 75 percent. And in 2006, less than 20 percent of REI's 170 retail management positions were filled from outside the organization. For eleven years straight, REI has been named one of *Fortune* magazine's 100 Best Companies to Work For.

While a majority of REI workers no doubt come to the company hardwired with a love of the outdoors, the sources of their on-the-job engagement extend beyond an inherent passion for sport and nature. The company's culture, its policies, and its executives' behavior play an enormous role. "Engagement is not so much a company program as a way of life," says Michelle Clements, REI's senior vice president of human resources. Employee research bears this out: the vast majority, 81 percent of workers, trust REI's leaders, agreeing that they're competent to run the business and sustain the company's stated values—authenticity, quality, service, respect, integrity, and balance. These and other perceptions contribute to what one employee called a "magical quality" that makes REI special. And it's this magical quality that inspires them to go above and beyond for customers and colleagues every day.

REI's engagement and financial success is in large part the result of a leadership quality to which many companies aspire but few achieve: inspiration. In the context of engagement, inspiration is the basis for workers' *emotional* attachment to their jobs and to the company, the "heart" part of engagement's three-part equation. So important is inspiration to achieving engagement that it comes through in three of the top ten engagement drivers identified in our *Global Workforce Study:*

- Senior management's sincere interest in employee well-being.
- The organization's reputation for social responsibility.
- Individuals' relationships with their supervisors.

Inspiration is the magic ingredient in the formula that leads employees to give discretionary effort freely and willingly, as if from the gut and without pause to question whether something is worth doing. While an organization's successful performance in and of itself can inspire us at some level—it feels good to be part of a winning team—day-to-day inspiration occurs largely through the connections an organization builds with all of its stakeholders. Specifically, how do people lead and communicate? What do leaders emphasize in interactions with employees, customers, investors, and the communities in which they operate? How do company managers and supervisors communicate with direct reports? Are messages direct and genuine or filtered and spun? What examples do leaders set, and what messages do their own behaviors convey in terms of what matters most? How do they delegate responsibility? What do they attend to, and what do they ignore?

Inspiration is the most intangible element in the quest for engagement. Unlike training courses, recognition awards, or annual bonuses, inspiration is not something we can touch or see, or that managers can buy or "assign" to others. Because it's so intangible, inspiration is often something managers appreciate when they observe it, but don't readily know what conscious actions they can take to create it. If a leader is "inspiring," it's easy to assume that he or she possesses some innate, charismatic gift that cannot be replicated. While some people seem to be inherently inspiring in their attitude, presence, vision, ideas, and communication style— think Apple's Steve Jobs or Virgin's Richard Branson—there are inspiring actions that any manager can take to bring about greater employee engagement.

In the following pages, we isolate just such behaviors. They stem from the insights gleaned from our *Global Workforce Study*—what thousands of employees told us inspires and engages them—as well as from our experiences interacting with many remarkably inspiring leaders, and from one-on-one interviews with the Engaging Eight organizations. During these interviews, if leaders or employees used the word *inspire,* we pushed for explanations and examples. Ultimately, we heard examples of inspiring behavior that went far beyond delivering a compelling speech.

Inspiration is not an emotional state that can be wished into existence. Nor can it be bottled, bought, or outsourced. But with effort and attention, you can create the so-called magic that sparks the hearts of REI workers. True engagement depends on it.

The Valued, Valuable Worker

To inspire, engaging companies create two key emotional bonds with employees: a sense of pride in the work they and the company do, and a belief that the company cares about their well-being. The former makes people feel that *their contributions are valued* highly by the organization and the larger community. The latter makes *them feel valuable.*

First, consider pride. People want to feel proud about *how* they earn a living, not just that they do earn a living. Knowing we have a positive effect on others gives us a sense of purpose, beyond the satisfaction we get from providing well for our families and ourselves. We want to feel proud when we tell friends, family, even potential employers where we work, what we do, and what our companies do. Indeed, people at all levels respond when their jobs hold a sense of purpose that comes from contributing to a larger cause or outcome they support, in addition to bringing home a paycheck.

A strong sense of pride in what we do for a living inspires us to do our personal best and to surpass our past achievements. To elicit pride among workers, organizations must do four complementary things:

1. Run a successful operation.
2. Espouse and embody self-declared values that dictate how people should conduct business.
3. Be a good, if not great, corporate citizen.
4. Cultivate a "brag-worthy" corporate reputation.

In addition to inspiration through pride, employees are inspired when they perceive that their organization's leaders are genuinely interested in their well-being as individuals and when they have good relationships with their supervisors. This point is crucially important and should not be underestimated. We'll dissect this idea in some detail later in the chapter. For now, suffice it to say that senior leaders as well as supervisors must consistently embrace the following behaviors:

- Manage with empathy, honesty, and visibility.
- Model stated values and standards of behavior.
- Create and encourage employees to use programs and policies that address workers' needs beyond the office.

In our *Global Workforce Study*, we discovered the following gaps in these areas:

- Only 49 percent of employees believe their senior leaders act in ways consistent with the organization's values.
- Only 38 percent say their senior management has a sincere interest in employees' well-being.
- Only 38 percent feel that their senior management communicates openly and honestly.
- Just 44 percent agree that senior management tries to be visible and accessible.

Direct bosses also fall short. Only 44 percent of employees agree that their direct bosses "inspire enthusiasm for work." In addition, only 57 percent say their immediate managers treat employees with trust and respect; only 51 percent say direct managers communicate clearly and openly; and only 43 percent say their direct bosses understand what motivates them as individuals.

These data underscore one thing: *organizations are not yet inspiring workers to the degree possible or necessary.*

To do so, the best and most effective leaders and managers possess a dual leadership competency that combines hard skills (financial, marketing, and operational prowess) with so-called soft skills (emotional and social intelligence, listening abilities, empathy, and humility). A CEO may have a winning strategic vision or a gift for running an efficient business operation, but he won't generate the success that is possible unless he can also touch people's hearts with his character and values. Executives are just beginning to fully appreciate the need to combine their business prowess and intelligence with these inspiring, engaging skills.

The Power of Pride

Below is a closer look at the four ways organizations successfully engender a sense of pride in their workforce.

RUN A SUCCESSFUL OPERATION

Employees want to work for organizations and leaders who are committed to, and focused on, long-term success. When leaders meet financial goals and outline well-crafted strategic plans for the future, workers feel a baseline sense of stability that frees them to focus on their jobs rather than on fear for the future of those jobs. Few things

are as distracting or as worrying as a sinking stock price or impending layoffs.

EMC's standing as the highest market-share revenue generator
in its industry is a tremendous source of pride—and engagement—
for its highly ambitious workforce; these are people who have high
expectations for themselves and thus the organizations with which
they associate. "I love handing people my EMC business card," says
twenty-four-year-old Kyle Leciejewski, a recently promoted regional
business manager in Chicago. His colleague, Stephen Todd—who
has been a tremendous source of innovation for EMC—mirrors the
sentiment: "I enjoy that my company is number one. It's fun to play
for the best team."

Engaging leaders do not rely on hyperbolic cheerleading to rouse
the workforce. They let performance speak for itself. That means
they communicate past successes, articulate future plans clearly,
even explain rather than ignore failures. The medium doesn't
matter; all-staff voice mails, e-mails, and in-person town hall–style
calls or gatherings can all be effective.

EMC's founder, Dick Egan, had a ritual of bringing all employees
together under one roof every quarter for a meeting where he would
run through the company's strategy and the goals for the given
quarter and coming year. Today, CEO Joe Tucci continues the
tradition. His discussion is frank and his purpose twofold: make it
clear to everyone—not just the C-suite or the salespeople—what's
expected of them, and rally the troops. At a recent EMC quarterly
meeting, some 6,000 Massachusetts-based employees gathered in
a giant warehouse to hear a series of messages designed to inspire
as well as inform. CEO Tucci discussed quarterly earnings (up 33
percent from the prior quarter). HR head Jack Mollen revealed
results of the latest employee survey (what employees felt good

about, as well as what they didn't). The room grew silent when an executive talked about a young EMC employee who passed away and showed a tribute video, sparking tears throughout the group. The mood shifted when the head of corporate communications announced EMC's logo would appear on Boston Red Sox uniforms—a first in Major League Baseball history—and then raffled off a large-screen TV and Patriot-themed gifts. This mix of information and inspiration is no accident. Says HR head Mollen, "Instilling a sense of pride in the company has been a vital part of EMC's HR transformation. We have to create a company that allows people to really feel good about the type of work they're doing and the people they're working with. If we can't accomplish that, then we'll lose some great talent."

Operating a successful business entails explaining to workers what's required to achieve winning results in the future. Business knowledge, in and of itself, can also inspire and increase the chances of successful performance. For example, look at REI. The retailer's bimonthly newsletters include a column titled "REI by the Numbers," which breaks down business basics for employees. Here's an excerpt from the March/April 2007 newsletter:

> It's spring, and new inventory is streaming into the Distribution Center [DC] and stores. This year, we'll spend $750 million on products to stock stores and REI.com. The difference between the amount we pay for an item and the amount we eventually sell it for—after subtracting costs such as shipping, shrinkage, and markdowns—is called gross margin. Say we buy a jacket from The North Face for $48. Our shipping cost is $2. The full retail price of the jacket is $100. But a customer uses a coupon to buy it for $80. Considering the shipping cost, we really sold

the jacket for $78. We end up with a gross margin of 38.5 percent on the jacket. Gross margin (GM) is a closely watched figure, and it varies from product to product. For 2007, our company-wide goal is an overall GM of 44.7 percent. Why is this number important for REI?

As we work toward $1.3 billion in sales this year, even a slight fluctuation in our GM means a huge difference in our earnings. Just one-tenth of 1 percent means a difference of $1.3 million in annual profits.

Everyone at REI plays a part in boosting our GM. Sourcing and DC teams manage transit costs. Merchants set product prices and time markdowns. Marketing and online teams drive traffic, and retail moves the sale. Efficient shipping and receiving teams lower shrinkage, as do alert sales specialists and finance teams who catch paperwork errors.

Communication such as this not only informs, it energizes. In addition to referring to work groups as "teams," it recognizes that workers at all levels can understand REI's business, while simultaneously explaining business basics for people who haven't had formal business training.

Employees resent being talked down to or spun, and such behavior can sever emotional bonds. But when given credit as capable to understand, people feel emotionally driven to deliver what they now know is required to be a winning organization. REI general manager Rachel Ligtenberg, who has overseen seven years of successive sales and earnings growth in her store, confirms this: "Our employees have a huge influence over our success, and the more informed every team member is, the more passionate they are to contribute to our success. People feel respected and included in our success when they at least know our goals."

ESPOUSE AND EMBODY SELF-DECLARED VALUES THAT DICTATE HOW TO CONDUCT BUSINESS

Employees want to take pride in *how* the organization and its leaders deliver on the strategic vision and achieve success—through their individual actions as well as through policies senior leaders set. Are administrative assistants treated with respect? Do overseas factory workers receive a fair and living wage? Does the company honor diversity at all levels? Do factories minimize pollution? Answers to these questions belie corporate values—values that dictate acceptable and unacceptable behaviors and provide guidelines that help individual employees make the best choices on a daily basis. Corporate values dictate the way all stakeholders in the company are treated, including customers, suppliers, employees, and shareholders. Behavior-guiding values are the building blocks of corporate culture, defining the level of focus on such things as safety and quality, customer service, efficiency, diversity, and creativity.

Values also unify disparate organizations, transcending differences and establishing common ground among distinct groups. While there is a set of core values, such as integrity and respect, that should be universally embraced in any business in any environment, other values need to be defined and communicated within the unique context of the organization, its strategy, how it operates, and what behaviors will yield the highest level of performance relative to the strategy. As we saw in chapter 1, close alignment among business strategy, annual goals, and cultural and workplace attributes is critical in creating an engaging work environment. For example, companies that differentiate themselves on product and service innovation most effectively deliver on that strategy when they have corresponding values of diversity and agility in the workplace. By contrast, companies competing primarily on excellent customer service need to focus on values and processes like collaboration, autonomy, and local flexibility.

The following are examples of guiding values at some of the Engaging Eight organizations:

- Honeywell International established what's known internally as the "12 Honeywell Behaviors," meant to guide employees' actions. The behaviors, in Honeywell's own parlance, are: growth and customer focus; leadership impact; gets results; makes people better; champions change and Six Sigma; fosters teamwork and diversity; global mind-set; takes intelligent risks; self-aware/learner; effective communicator; integrative thinker; and technical or functional excellence. Employees, including the chief executive, are evaluated on what they achieve as well as how they perform against each of the twelve behaviors.

- At Campbell, the company's three stated values are character, competence, and teamwork. CEO Doug Conant regularly speaks to employee groups about the three values in the context of his favorite mantra: to win in the marketplace, we must win in the workplace. Every six weeks, Conant talks about those values for about thirty minutes at the company's new-employee meetings. He also discusses them over luncheons that he holds for some twenty to thirty workers, from administrative assistants to managers. A few days before our interview, Conant preached his philosophy at a Pepperidge Farm sales meeting. Employees find Conant's words and themes remarkably consistent and, over time, his words have gained traction in the culture.

- McKesson's five Shared Principles are expressed through the acronym I-CARE: integrity, customer first, accountability, respect, and excellence. CEO John Hammergren discusses the Shared Principles at town hall meetings that he holds with approximately half of the company's employees every year. McKesson also tracks how well leaders are "living" the values by measuring their employees' perception of them on engagement surveys.

- Novartis's global leadership team identified ten guiding behaviors on which employees are evaluated. Scores for these qualitative measures carry as much weight as the quantitative financial measures used to determine bonuses at the end of each year. Novartis's values are: customer and quality focus; innovation and creativity; competence, results driven; leadership; action oriented and simplicity; empowerment and accountability; commitment; mutual respect; integrity; and open communication.

- EMC's credo is practical, identifying priorities and specific behaviors it expects. Says EMC, "We are a leading technology company that is driven to perform, to partner, to execute. We go about our jobs with a passion for delivering results that exceed our customers' expectations for quality, service, innovation, and interaction. We pride ourselves on doing what's right and putting our customers' best interests first. We lead change and change to lead. We are devoted to advancing our people, our customers, industry, and community. We say what we mean and do what we say. We are EMC, where information lives."

Whether dubbed values, principles, or expected behaviors, such guidelines are all variations on a key theme: *how a company reaches its goals is as important as the goals themselves.*

Of course, talk from the top is cheap unless leaders themselves embody the values they espouse, even when only one person is watching.

At REI, CEO Jewell closely observes how colleagues and job candidates talk to her assistant, the receptionist, and others when they visit her office. On occasion, Jewell has expressed her disappointment to people who show anything less than respect to her "teammates." Adds Jewell, "People know I will not accept it." At MGM Grand, people also know that President Gamal Aziz does not like petty behavior. From day one he's been quick to cut people off the moment they start gossiping about coworkers. "They know that behavior is not tolerated inside or outside of my office," says Aziz, adding, "the way I treat people who report directly to me [affects] the way they treat others. I want to hear about legitimate problems, like unethical behavior, but my goal is to create an environment of support and team spirit."

He's correct. Behaviors and values flow down. That's why Aziz thanks his secretary at the end of each day and tries to smile at everyone he passes as he walks down the long corridor from his office to the main casino floor. "I know what it feels like not to have the boss say hello," he says. The ripple effects are real. Listen to what MGM Grand's Michael Solas, who works in the payroll department, has to say about his bosses: "There's always a good morning, always a smile, they never ignore me . . ."

Often, it's small gestures that symbolize what matters most to leaders. Unscripted behaviors—even the order in which a CEO talks about corporate priorities—carry symbolic weight. During the course of our discussions with Engaging Eight employees, almost all referred to his or her company's chief executive officer by first name: Doug, Gamal, Sally, Michael. This policy of informality does not provoke disrespect for the head of the organization in most cultures, but rather conveys a sense that the boss is approachable.

BE A GOOD, EVEN GREAT, CORPORATE CITIZEN

REI is not just in the business of selling backpacks, tents, hiking boots, and outerwear. Its stated mission is more ambitious: "to inspire, educate and outfit for a lifetime of outdoor adventure and stewardship." As part of its business plan, REI supports a myriad of regional and global philanthropic initiatives that reflect this commitment. Each year, for example, REI donates a portion of its operating profits, in the form of grants, to help protect and restore the environment, increase access to outdoor activities, and encourage involvement in responsible outdoor recreation. Employees can nominate organizations, projects, and programs in which they are personally involved to receive funding or donations. In 2006 alone, REI granted $4 million to more than 430 community groups. Managers also are given eight hours of paid community outreach time, and each store employs at least one person dedicated to community outreach.

Companies' commitment to larger social issues—to making a meaningful difference in the wider world and addressing the sustainability of the planet—has become an increasingly important element for employees everywhere. Recall, for instance, that in our *Global Workforce Study,* corporate social responsibility ranked as the third most significant driver of engagement among all employees worldwide.

But what, exactly, does the term mean?

As defined by the Center for Corporate Citizenship—a twenty-year-old nonprofit research and educational body associated with

Boston College's Carroll School of Management—corporate citizenship and social responsibility is the business strategy that shapes the values underpinning a company's mission and the choices made each day by its executives, managers, and employees as they engage with society. Good corporate citizens commit to "minimizing harm" to employees, customers, communities, and the environment. For example, they ensure employee safety and operate eco-friendly factories that reduce carbon emissions. Good corporate citizens also try to "maximize benefit" through such things as participating to solve education and youth development issues, paying fair wages, or producing a product with a social value. Good corporate citizens strive to earn trust with transparent communications and business practices while, at the same time, recognizing that making money is part of their obligation to society and their investors, as well as to their employees.

Note that corporate citizenry is not just about randomly donating large sums of money to a pet project. As REI's environmental efforts demonstrate, there can and should be a strategic connection to an organization's charitable mission and business.

For many organizations, their fundamental products or services inherently provide employees with a sense of what we call pride-in-product. For example, employees at three Engaging Eight companies—global health care company Novartis, wholesale health care supply and service company McKesson, and hospital network North Shore–Long Island Jewish Health System—repeatedly said that a main reason they choose to work in the health care field despite its many challenges is because the field affords opportunities to make significant, life-altering changes for people. We heard this refrain from CEOs, administrators, managers, researchers, and plant managers alike.

Thomas Hughes is the global head of the Cardiovascular and

Metabolism Disease Area at Novartis's Institutes for Biomedical Research. Hughes has been with the company for two decades, and he talks about the pride that comes from knowing that his on-the-job, problem-solving duties have real-life applications. Says Hughes, "For us it is about patients. We are here to identify ways to bring new benefit to people who are suffering from diseases." Yet, despite the feel-good factor embedded in Hughes's daily efforts, he and his colleagues face a harsh reality in that the true fruits of their drug innovation and development labors—healing the sick—are usually not realized for years. Even if a drug they invent succeeds at treating disease, it takes an average of ten to fifteen years to get a new drug from laboratory to market, according to the Tufts Center for the Study of Drug Development. So where do employees such as Hughes find short-term inspiration? What keeps them engaged on a daily basis, even when the inspiring promise is so far off in the future? As Hughes explains, an organization's extracurricular corporate citizenry can make all the difference:

> People who interview here ask me that all the time, and it comes in a couple of different flavors. One thing about Novartis that is enchanting is the caliber of its top management. If you simply spend a few minutes looking at what Novartis stands for, it is about innovation and understanding the larger role the corporation plays in society, about having a reasonable balance in investments that will drive our own profitability and allow us to sustain our relationship with the external community and benefit the planet . . . the fact that we have the Novartis Institute for Tropical Diseases to [try to cure] leprosy and malaria and the Novartis Vaccines' Institute for Global Health to prevent other disabling diseases . . . not many companies would bother to do that systematically . . . the fact that the

output of our technology, know-how, and drug discovery skills can apply to problems affecting people outside of our traditional target populations, while at the same time make us more profitable, gives many of us a very good feeling.

In 2007, Novartis Pharma employees ranked corporate citizenship as the *second most important driver* contributing to their engagement, according to an internal survey of Pharma employees. The company's good works have positive repercussions at all levels of the organization. In 2005, Chief Executive Dr. Daniel Vasella committed Novartis to providing 30 million treatments (blister cards with anywhere from six to twenty-four tablets) of its malaria drug Coartem to the World Health Organization (WHO) by the end of the year. The WHO would acquire the drug at a significantly reduced cost and distribute it for free where it was needed most, mainly in Africa. Novartis exceeded its commitment and produced 33 million treatments in 2005. A bulk of the ambitious manufacturing and packaging project fell to the employees in the Suffern, New York, plant. The huge volume required the plant to almost double its daily output, install new machines, and reconfigure many areas of the plant over a five-month period, recalls one Suffern team facilitator, John Micheline.

"We were committed to getting it done," says Micheline, "for the children dying of malaria in Africa as well as for Dr. Vasella . . . he trusted the business as a whole to do it, and you do not make a commitment like that unless you trust the people."

Micheline and his colleagues made sure the plant workers understood the magnitude of malaria's deadly toll—more than 1 million people die of malaria every year, mostly infants, children, and pregnant women in Africa, according to the WHO. That information—as well as Vasella's faith in their ability to deliver—

inspired workers to do whatever it took to meet the year-end deadline. Dozens voluntarily put in unpaid overtime, even during the holiday season. "We could not force people to work, so we put up lists for volunteers," says Micheline. "We ended up finishing at eight p.m. on New Year's Eve. My boss took the whole team to a local restaurant to celebrate, and they took some photos of everyone and sent them to Dr. Vasella on Monday morning." Vasella responded to the e-mail personally, congratulating the plant employees. The company continued to increase the number of Coartem treatments for distribution to patients in need. In 2006, 62 million treatments worth $179 million were delivered. In 2007, 66 million treatments worth $190 million were delivered. In total, Novartis contributed $937 million worth of treatments in 2007 through a variety of access-to-medicine programs, reaching 66 million people in need.

Not every company is in the business of saving lives, and corporate citizenry must be even more pronounced when the core product or service is not inherently altruistic or philanthropic. An extreme example among the Engaging Eight would be Las Vegas's MGM Grand, whose revenue comes primarily from entertainment. Its year-round charitable activities create a focus on altruism that its daily business operations—from dealing blackjack to providing food, lodging, and entertainment to cleaning rooms—may not otherwise induce. "The culture of giving that MGM Grand has established helps employees feel that there is a larger purpose to their jobs beyond serving customers. It lends a greater level of pride to the job," says Miriam Hammond, MGM Grand's senior vice president of human resources, who came to MGM Grand in 2001 from the health care industry.

MGM Grand brings in more than $1 billion in revenues for its parent company, MGM Mirage, and its charitable giving is substantial.

Each year, MGM Grand holds an eight-week fund-raiser in March and April to benefit churches, schools, animal foundations, and cancer research initiatives throughout southern Nevada. Between 1999 and 2005, thousands of MGM Grand employees raised a total of $6.7 million. In 2007, the company hit a new annual high when it raised $2 million. That's a tremendous achievement for less than 10,000 employees in just two months. In addition to pledging money, employees get involved by participating and helping to create fun fund-raising programs that are in the spirit of MGM Grand's core service. There are poker, blackjack, and craps tournaments; jewelry and book sales; live and silent auctions; and even lost-and-found sales of items that guests left at the hotel. One year, an employee suggested that each department create an Easter basket to be auctioned off. The company took the suggestion, and the event has become an annual tradition. In addition to the two-month fund-raiser, giving continues year-round with food, clothing, book, and blood drives.

MGM Grand also has ways for employees to help each other. The company's Employee Emergency Relief Fund gives financial assistance to workers who, for example, may need money to pay for a family member's funeral or rebuild after a house fire. During the holiday season, seventy-five MGM Grand employees' families considered "in-need" receive everything from Christmas trees to gift certificates and toys, all donated by colleagues.

The extensive culture of giving that permeates MGM Grand helps employees see themselves not just as purveyors of food, drink, and entertainment, but as valuable participants of an ongoing, philanthropic engine of sorts that transforms revenue into more than profits. No doubt, these efforts have also contributed to MGM Grand's broader reputation in the local and greater business communities.

Engaging leaders such as MGM Grand's Aziz and Novartis's Vasella are able to find and articulate connections between an organization's output—be it products such as life-saving drugs or by-products such as charitable giving—and a greater good. In turn, they tap an emotional chord with employees. Proof is in the worker population. MGM Grand's Bette Gaines-Snyder does not just see herself as the director of slot and employee events. Says Gaines-Snyder, who began her casino career as a show dancer, "We are a community serving a greater community. Just knowing that is a great source of pride."

CULTIVATE A BRAG-WORTHY CORPORATE REPUTATION

Values and corporate citizenship contribute to the organization's overall reputation among a variety of stakeholders, including customers, employees, investors, local communities, as well as the media. An organization's reputation reflects its perceived character, which aids in recruitment and retention efforts and significantly contributes to employee pride. People want to work and be part of winning, admired groups.

Our Engaging Eight organizations have been recognized as leaders for financial performance, for their workplaces, and for diversity, innovation, and public service. Among some of their awards: Campbell Soup Company, McKesson, and MGM Mirage (MGM Grand's parent company) have each been, or are currently, on *Fortune*'s prestigious list of Most Admired Companies in America. REI has been a *Fortune* Best Company to Work For eleven consecutive years and continues to win regional awards for public service. In 2007, Novartis ranked twenty-five among *Barron's* Most Respected Companies worldwide (it ranked twenty-three in 2006); Novartis is also one of *BusinessWeek*'s 50 Most Valuable Brands.

EMC earned a spot in *Wired* magazine's Top 40 and *BusinessWeek*'s InfoTech 100. Honeywell has been named as one of the Great Places to Work in India, a Top 50 Company for Women Engineers, and one of *Fortune*'s Most Admired companies in the aerospace and defense industry.

At the time Doug Conant became CEO, Campbell had devolved into what *BusinessWeek* called "a beleaguered old brand" as sales for the company's largest product line, condensed soups, had declined amid competition. The company restored the reputation of its iconic image among consumers, investors, and workers through new tactics such as improving the taste of its soups, creating easier-to-shop retail shelving, topping cans with easy-open lids, and unleashing fresh marketing campaigns. Today, the brand's revived respect resonates with employees such as Campbell's Mary Lemonis, director of global organizational effectiveness:

> For me, the reputation of the company, the brand, is a huge part of why I like my work. Campbell's is an icon brand; you tell people where you work and people tell you a story about their favorite soup or something, like if their mom used to give them Campbell's Chicken Noodle when they were sick as a child. I really believe in what we are doing, and Doug [Conant] is a fantastic sponsor.

Lemonis, who moved across the world from Australia to Philadelphia, Pennsylvania, to continue working for Campbell, is so loyal that she doesn't even buy competitive food products for her home. That said, inspiring reputations are not reserved for consumer brands with household names. Whatever the product or service—from ball gowns to ball bearings—employees can experience inspiration just by knowing that their organization executes in accordance with the highest standards. Again, EMC's Stephen Todd:

> I have a very strong respect for the storage products we build because they are often used in life-threatening situations. If someone is on an operating table and the doctor needs an X-ray, we want him to get the X-ray fast and have it be 100 percent accurate . . . the same can be said for someone using a bank account . . . our products shoulder a tremendously huge responsibility, and all EMC employees know that so we really are committed to the quality of the systems we ship.

Employees are driven in part by a corporate mission that prioritizes their customers. At MGM Grand, President Gamal Aziz encourages employees to look beyond their tactical responsibilities and to create a customer experience that allows guests to fully escape their everyday reality and be treated like royalty with world-class food, entertainment, accommodations, and service. Aziz branded the desired customer experience Maximum Vegas. MGM Grand's workers are encouraged to think of themselves as cohosts who work in concert to deliver the overall Maximum Vegas experience. A poolside server, for instance, is not just delivering cosmopolitans to sunbathers. A concierge is not just booking restaurant reservations for hotel guests. A chef is not just preparing a meal. Each is contributing to the Maximum Vegas promise to guests, helping ensure that the cocktail is delivered with a smile and refreshed before the guest even has to ask; that the time of the restaurant reservation coordinates with guests' concert tickets, giving them ample time to get to the theater for the 8 p.m. show; and that the meal reflects the diner's preferences and is presented like a work of art.

Delivering superior customer service is a cornerstone of many organizations' business strategy, and it is also a rallying call for engaged workers. While employees take pride in an organization dedicated to treating them well, they see an imperative when it comes to addressing and resolving customers' problems. As you will recall, in our *Global Workforce Study* employees ranked their organization's ability to "quickly resolve customer concerns" as the fifth most important factor that contributed to their engagement. When an organization has an infrastructure in place to adequately address customers' needs, employees can feel proud about the product or service they are helping to provide. In contrast, ignoring customers' problems and needs is tantamount to a crime that, in employees' eyes, is grounds for disengagement not only because it's not right, but because it may tarnish the organization's reputation and ultimately affect its success.

Reputation, as it is widely understood, takes years to establish but a moment to destroy. In recent history, the business world has witnessed once-respected companies come crashing down in ethical firestorms, unable to recover. Enron. Arthur Andersen. Tyco. Adelphia. Quest. WorldCom. Most senior leaders derail—and in some cases take their companies with them—not because of operational incompetence, but because they do not behave according to the type of overriding values we discussed earlier.

Financial success, values, corporate citizenry, and reputation fuel the virtuous cycle of high organizational performance and employee engagement. While it's impossible to determine which is the cause and which the outcome, we know that there is a very high positive quantitative correlation between the two variables. Simply put, when there is high employee engagement, there is usually also strong organizational performance and vice versa.

Show Sincere Interest in Employees

Inspiration also comes when employees believe that their organization's senior management is sincerely interested in their well-being. What does this mean?

First, employee *well-being* refers to a worker's whole self—his health, his family, his financial stability. Leaders demonstrate sincere interest in these aspects of an individual's life through a combination of informal communication and formal policies. Human beings come to the workplace with full lives beyond the office or plant walls. When they believe that their employer cares about that, they feel inspired to give more of that whole self to the company.

Second, leaders and managers need to take an *interest* in workers. This doesn't mean acting like a best friend or a therapist, but rather an attentive boss. In the context of the workplace, interest connotes a willingness to listen and consider workers' unique needs and motivations. Interest means taking time to understand what an individual does every day in his or her job. Interest requires leaders to develop a thorough appreciation of how organizational changes affect people's lives at work and outside work. Interest can be demonstrated via one-on-one interaction as well as through the company-wide programs and policies that are put in place.

Leaders' interest must also be *sincere*. People easily detect the difference between scripted and genuine attention, and between corporate programs that deliver real benefits and those that just look good in an annual report. They know if there's a long-term commitment or if the action is merely a temporary opportunity for leaders to look good. Sincerity also involves follow-through. It requires leaders to understand why they need to keep employees' well-being top of mind. It can't be playacting or employees will see right through it.

Finally, this all starts, and ends, with senior leaders—not just direct bosses. There is still a popular myth that engagement is primarily an individual manager's responsibility. No doubt, first-line managers play a role, but they can't effectively do their jobs unless senior leaders set the stage. Today's flatter, dispersed organizational structures mean that employees are more self-directed and empowered than in the past. They also have more access than ever before to hear, see, and communicate with the executive team. Because today's chief executives, in particular, play such a public role and personify the organizations they lead, they have an unprecedented amount of power to communicate with and thus inspire the workforce.

MANAGE WITH EMPATHY, HONESTY, AND VISIBILITY

While leaders need not bare their souls to connect, employees are inspired when leaders exhibit a genuine ability to understand and identify with others' feelings, issues, and unique styles.

Empathy is a prerequisite for inspiration. While some leaders associate empathy with treating workers too softly, we have seen that engaging leaders can be empathetic and simultaneously maintain high performance standards. We believe people are even more inspired to perform well for leaders who combine high expectations with the ability to listen and respond to workers' needs.

Empathy requires a leader to envision how it would feel to walk in someone else's shoes. EMC's Bonnie Bryce, a senior manager in global marketing and single mother whose son has significant special needs, describes how her boss of ten years, Frank Hauck, does so:

He is truly a genuinely kind, good person who treats people
with respect. He cares. And he listens. As a leader you need to
relate to people on a personal level. And he does . . . Frank has
been so accommodating with my schedules. I have talked to so
many people, and they all adore him because he's approachable and listens. Frank is great at just stopping by the office,
asking how it's going, or if he sees you're a little distressed, he
just sort of lets you know he's there . . . he doesn't forget to say
"thank you." If he recognizes something I did, you better believe I want to work harder. That means more than money.

Hauck's response, when asked to describe his management style,
showed discipline goes hand in hand with his sensitivity:

I have to be willing to make the same personal sacrifices and
commitments I expect others to make. Second, I have to give
people invigorating things to do; they have to feel good and
challenged about how they spend their day. And then I have to
set goals and objectives, and hold them accountable. Managing is like parenting in the sense that what you really want to
do is give people roots and then wings; build into them the
same values and discipline that you have, and over time allow
them to grow.

Workers also feel valued when even the highest-placed executives
"get" their world. It's easy for busy, pressured executives to forget
where they came from as they become more and more removed
from day-to-day operations, but employees respond to leaders who
can identify with them—or at least those who make an honest effort
to try.

North Shore–LIJ's chief Michael Dowling often prefers to meet with union members without his executive entourage. Explains Dowling, "[Employees] want to believe that I am sincere, someone to be trusted and real. Executives hide behind titles, but having a title does not make a leader. I want them to trust me for what I represent, not my title. I want them to feel comfortable coming up and talking to me." Because Dowling grew up working plumbing and construction jobs, he judiciously shares this personal history with workers in similar situations. "I do not gloat about it," says Dowling, "but at the appropriate time I say, 'Let me tell you what I did thirty years ago . . . I worked with a shovel, and I understand you pretty well.'"

Leaders who cannot identify firsthand with workers from personal experience should admit it. For example, they can tell workers that they will never fully grasp what it takes to haul a heavy pallet full of boxes, write a press release, or make a collection call, but visiting workers on the job gives the executive a better appreciation for the hard work they do. If employees never see C-suite executives out and about—walking the halls, eating in the cafeteria, even manning the cash register—then whatever strategic vision management puts forth is not as likely to carry much emotional weight.

At Campbell, Jerry Buckley, senior vice president of public affairs, recalls Doug Conant's first day at the company as CEO. "Doug stood up in the cafeteria and said, 'I know that it is absolutely unrealistic for us to ask you to uniquely honor our organization . . . and to demonstrate an extraordinary commitment to our success . . . until we have demonstrated that same level of commitment to you and your success. You see, I know that in order to win in the marketplace, we need to first win in the workplace.'" That speech, says Buckley, became the basis of what came to be known as the Campbell Promise: Campbell Valuing People, People Valuing Campbell. In the weeks following his cafeteria speech, Conant's efforts to connect got more personal as he met one-on-one with members of his executive team, sharing information about himself and encouraging others to do the same. It's difficult to show sincere interest without showing up, in person and face-to-face. Says EMC's CEO Joe Tucci:

> You have to get out there. When I travel I always do two things: see customers and see our people. I may or may not meet press or investors, but I always, always sit down with our people informally and talk.

Employees notice. Kyle Leciejewski says he "almost lost it" when he was introduced to "Joe" on his third day with the company. "My boss's boss pulled [Joe] over and I shook his hand . . . there's a respect for human capital here, to use an HR term, that's evident in how accessible executives are. They don't stand in a cluster at events, and they share things they hear back up the chain of command."

Recall how North Shore–LIJ CEO Michael Dowling attends all new-employee meetings. This action inspires project director Carol Merkel:

> I have a very high regard for Michael Dowling. What first impressed me? He attends every single weekly new-employee orientation meeting; not every CEO does that, and it is a great representation of what North Shore is all about. He sets an example; he says, "I am here because I want to be, and you are here because you want to be, and together we can do good work."

Engaging executives sometimes use town hall meetings— semiorchestrated events to speak to and hear from groups of employees in informal settings. One division of Novartis, Exploratory

Clinical Development, whose 1,000 employees translate scientific research into new therapies, has perfected the town hall tactic. The division's former head, Trevor Mundel (he is currently global head of development functions), insists that each member of his executive team meet with three or four employee groups throughout the year. But to ensure that the leaders do more than just chat idly with workers, Mundel insists they identify one obstacle that prevents each group from accomplishing its goals and then develop an action plan to fix it. "Employees must not just see that [a senior executive] listened to them, but that something came out of it," says Mundel. Often, all it takes is a phone call from someone on Mundel's team to ease, say, a bureaucratic bottleneck plaguing a particular group of workers. Mundel's town halls have won rave reviews from employees.

Empathy, transparency, and visibility are the unwritten rules of interested, engaging leaders. Together, they help employees feel that leaders care about their well-being.

Support Programs and Policies That Care for Workers' Needs Beyond the Office

Back at Novartis's 160-acre plant in Suffern, New York, more than 400 employees package billions of tablets annually for maladies such as hypertension and malaria. John Micheline has been with Novartis eighteen years, and the forty-two-year-old father of four prides himself on being a successful, inspiring team facilitator, able to walk the line between supporting his associates personally and upholding professional expectations. It is a balance he has been able to maintain with help from his employer:

> I always have to be ready for anything because every day is something totally new. We have all walks of life here, over

three shifts. You deal with other people's issues. There is a big trust factor involved. People start opening up not only about work-related issues but personal issues, too . . . I get close enough where they work harder for me . . . from a motivational standpoint . . . one of the fundamental characteristics of a good manager is listening, and by that I mean allowing people to explain themselves; when they do, there is an unconscious sense that "[my boss] supports me, he is there for me." If they see that I am there to help them, or if they have an issue about our work environment, such as safety, and they see I take action to address it, then they see I care. Depending on how my relationship is with the person, I [find] the comfort zone. I know I can reel it back when I have to.

Some issues—such as a death in the family or mental health issues—can affect employees' performance but are beyond any manager's ability and responsibility to address. When workers' personal problems prove to be more than Micheline has the time or training to deal with, he refers people to Novartis's employee assistance program (EAP)—an outsourced, anonymous counseling service that's common at most large organizations. Micheline says his ability to suggest that some workers use the company's EAP program—which he himself has used—is a "tool in his management arsenal."

The direct boss may be the closest opportunity a worker has to connect emotionally to the organization, but the boss cannot be the only one responsible to care for and show interest in a worker's well-being, no matter how empathetic or good at listening he or she may be. The organization and its senior management can also show they care about employees by instituting formal work-life balance programs. By doing so, the employers are essentially telling workers that they care about their physical, financial, and emotional well-being outside the walls of the company. Top among workers' priorities these days is flexibility—flexibility to deal with the unexpected, and flexibility to accommodate special routines needed for unique personal situations.

Consider the flexibility afforded EMC's Tracey Doyle. Among her responsibilities is to increase customer satisfaction ratings. Not only have those scores improved as part of her work, but one process improvement her team initiated will save EMC more than $150 million over the next five years. Doyle could not have performed so well if EMC did not honor and accommodate her very unique life situation. She is married, as well as the full-time guardian for a forty-five-year-old man with developmental disabilities whom she met in her former career as a health care worker. Caring for David requires Doyle to leave work for his doctor appointments, clinician meetings, and unexpected emergencies.

> EMC has been so successful helping me balance what I need to do to help David. He was hospitalized three years ago. My boss offered to drive me to the hospital and supported me when I needed to stay there for a while. Whenever David has a doctor's appointment I am able to flex my time to help him health-wise. David has also been included in various EMC events . . . My peers and management recognize him as an integral part of my family, not just as his guardian. That makes it much easier for me to support David. The company knows I will be flexible right back. I don't mind putting in time and working long hours because I know I will get it back when I need to.

We'll discuss the flexibility issue in more detail in chapter 6, but below is a partial list of programs offered at many Engaging Eight organizations. These program's communicate the company's interest in employees' well-being—their health, their financial stability, and their lives beyond work.

- Regularly scheduled health care fairs that offer free flu shots, blood pressure screenings, as well other health tests.
- Free, twenty-four-hour access to nurses via an 800-number.
- Flextime policies so managers and workers can customize schedules to fit the needs of employees who must care for children or elders.
- On-site fitness centers.
- On-site child care centers.
- Free or subsidized cafeteria meals with healthy menu options.
- Financial assistance for employees' children.
- Smoking cessation and weight-loss courses.
- Personal financial counseling.

For employees like single mother Shannon Johnson, a thirty-six-year-old table games dealer at MGM Grand, these types of policies and programs create a system of personal support that make her feel like her company cares. In the fall of 2007, Johnson began taking a casino management class, which MGM Grand is helping to pay for, that conflicted with her work hours. Her boss willingly accommodated a schedule change, allowing Johnson to come in an hour later—after her class was over—and stay an hour later. On top of this, Johnson is learning to speak Spanish on MGM Grand's dime. She has also used several other MGM Grand programs to address her personal situation. For example, she and her daughter attend six free counseling sessions together each year, and she uses the convenient MGM Grand facility for child care when she's working and her daughter is not at school. Johnson also lost thirty pounds in a Weight Watchers program for which MGM Grand reimbursed her. She took the corporate smoking-cessation class and quit.

Taken together, these programs send a very powerful message to employees like Shannon Johnson. She believes her company not only understands and empathizes with her personal situation, but is also willing to invest in things that will enable her to thrive at work and beyond. Says Johnson, "Women have their own challenges as primary care givers, and I feel MGM Grand is very flexible with me." Most important, she says, "I feel well taken care of."

In Closing: The Inspired Employee

Once, after visiting one of REI's warehouses and meeting its employees, chief executive Sally Jewell was leaving the building with a colleague who mentioned the name of one worker who impressed her. Jewell, who realized she had not said hello to that particular employee, ran back into the warehouse to find him. At REI, the CEO's sincere efforts to inspire by connecting to the workforce trickle down the ranks.

Recall that the head of REI's flagship store in Seattle, Rachel Ligtenberg, knows the names—and then some—of most of the store's 442 employees. Her interest in people matters to employees such as Duy Tran. When Tran first joined REI from the Peace Corps, he told Ligtenberg he wasn't interested in a long-term career in retail because he wanted to do something more altruistic. Undeterred, Ligtenberg went out of her way to tell Tran the various ways that the store supported Seattle's community groups, including the eight hours of paid community work per quarter that REI gives managers. Says Tran, "[My boss] encouraged and allowed me to continue to volunteer at a nonprofit called Bike Works, and I eventually became a board member." When a position opened to head REI flagship store's community outreach efforts, Ligtenberg brought Tran into her office and convinced him that the position would be a great opportunity to combine his professional skills and personal interests.

Says Tran, "That was two years ago, and it's been amazing and rewarding ever since. Sally always comes by and talks to us, so I see her all the time, and she shares ideas and listens to mine." Tran has adopted Jewell's and Ligtenberg's inspiring management styles as his own.

What workers want, after their basic financial and physical needs are met, is a degree of emotional fulfillment. We all want to be inspired, and we can be when our work has a worthy purpose that extends beyond self-interest, and when we believe our employer is interested in our well-being. It feels good to know that our work can improve the lives of others—customers, colleagues, our own direct reports—while at the same time our employer cares enough to help us improve our own lives.

Every organization has the power to make employees feel valuable and valued. Indeed, Abraham Maslow's hierarchy of needs theory plays out in the workplace. Fill people's wallets and they will do their jobs; fill their hearts and they will do much, much more.

5

Involve Them

Inform Employees, Gather Their Input, and Encourage Collaboration

Give people a place to make a difference, and it's
amazing what they can get done.
—Dave Cote, CEO, Honeywell International

n 2002, Honeywell International was reeling from years of up-
heaval that included a complex merger with Allied-Signal, followed by a tumultuous bidding war, and a failed takeover bid by
GE. A year earlier, Honeywell reported a net loss of $99 million on
revenues of $23.6 billion, reflecting a turbulent year and one-time
charges for divestitures and various operating improvements. To
salvage the situation, Dave Cote—the former chairman and CEO of
TRW Inc. and former GE senior vice president—was named CEO
and president of the multibillion-dollar maker of aerospace products, automotive parts, control technologies, and chemicals.

Cote's strategy included a concentrated effort to integrate
Honeywell's disparate business units and standardize internal work
processes for more efficiency and better margins, which he believed
could only be achieved with more involvement from front-line
workers in Honeywell's manufacturing sites. To that end, Cote and
his executive team created the Honeywell Operating System (HOS),
a method to manage its supply chain that, like the renowned Toyota

Production System, standardizes certain work flows, reduces waste, and helps solve problems faster so results for safety, quality, delivery, cost, and inventory are as close to exceptional as humanly possible.

The problem-solving aspect of the Honeywell Operating System reflects one of Cote's favored philosophies, that "great people organized and motivated in the right way can transcend bad processes and even bad strategies." In other words, Cote believes the way to fix ineffective processes is to have employees actively help define the best way to get work done. In Cote's view, valuable ideas to improve departmental, plant, or group performance can and should come from anyone—including supervisors, shop floor workers, and administrative assistants. Enabling people to help solve problems not only makes it possible for good ideas to blossom, but also makes employees feel more connected and keen to give their all.

In companies as large as Honeywell—with its 125,000 employees in more than 100 countries—involvement starts at the ground level, with line workers. A specific example of the impact of involving employees in process improvement efforts can be seen at a midsize Honeywell chemical manufacturing plant in Muskegon, Michigan, that produces complex chemicals for industry and pharmaceutical use. Each product is unique in its complexity, and customers won't hesitate to find another supplier if their orders are not delivered on time and defect-free. In 2005, plant manager David Price was brought in to make the facility more nimble and improve worker safety, product quality, and on-time delivery. He had his work cut out for him; at the time he joined, plant workers often had no clue whether projects were even running on schedule. Recalls Price:

> Our challenge was to get to a point where people knew exactly
> what they had to do when they walked on to the shop floor in

the morning . . . we had to change the way the plant runs. It used to be that people got their goals from on high and got marching orders from the next level. We changed that and now we plan in a more employee-focused way. As management, we also try to explain to shop floor workers how the world has changed and why the way of doing things for twenty years is no longer good enough. We let them know if a new competitor has emerged. We tell them how customers' expectations are changing and explain why we need to reduce costs. When people know what is going on at the company, when they see the numbers on a daily basis, even if those numbers are going the wrong way, it's a whole lot better than just seeing bad numbers at the end of the month and wondering why they did not know sooner so they could have a chance to steer the ship in the right direction.

When you take people's advice, you also have to involve them in making change happen. That can be scary for employees. It stretches folks. Some people look at that with suspicion and assume management will do it their way anyway. Others love being asked their opinion. Make no mistake, actively involving employees is a never-ending journey, but it's imperative for success.

Since Price took over, the plant's workforce is more informed and involved, as we'll see firsthand later in this chapter. From a results standpoint, the Muskegon plant has achieved measurable improvements. It went from as many as four worker injuries a year to none in 2007. That year was also the plant's best product-quality year on record, with the number of product defects down 80 percent from 2005 to mid-2007. On-time product delivery dates—which used to be negotiated, but are now set at the customers' desired time no matter how short the lead time—are also up. In 2007, 92 percent of the plant's orders were delivered on time, compared to 87 percent the previous year. Underlying the Muskegon plant's success are the types of employee involvement that Cote pushes for throughout Honeywell: the need to keep employees informed, to invite their opinions, and provide freedom to solve problems and collaborate.

Under CEO Cote, Honeywell continues to prosper. In 2007, cash flow from operations increased 22 percent to $3.9 billion on sales of $34.6 billion, which were up 10 percent from the previous year.

Emphasizing employee involvement is by no means the sole secret to Honeywell's continued success, yet aspects of employee involvement came up in almost every conversation we had with people at the company, from the CEO to a Denver secretary to a senior manager in India. In the following pages, we look at how Honeywell and other Engaging Eight organizations boost engagement via informing, gathering input, and giving employees the freedom to act. In others words, by involving people.

The Knowledgeable Worker

In the context of engagement, employee involvement is a prerequisite. One of the top five engagement drivers globally is employees' ability to provide input into decision making in their department, according to our *Global Workforce Study*. Not surprisingly, this also shows up as a key engagement driver in the United States, taking shape as a desire for appropriate decision-making power to do the job well.

There's more to "input" than meets the eye. It's not just about an employee being able to proffer an opinion now and again. Ideally, workers want to offer knowledge-based input that will be taken seriously and has the potential to make a real difference. Indeed, the tenth engagement driver—the organization encourages innovative thinking—suggests that employees want an opportunity to be innovative and to have an outlet for their creative ideas.

In short, employees want to be actively involved in their organizations—on both the receiving and giving end of information and ideas.

What distinguishes involvement at Honeywell and other engaging organizations, however, is that there's meaningful action behind the words. Unless involvement has real teeth—meaning employees really have information and power to shape or make a decision—it can quickly devolve into the somewhat meaningless "empowerment" mantra of the late 1980s and early 1990s, promoting cynicism, not engagement.

To ensure their genuine involvement, employees must be knowledgeable participants, treated as valued contributors, and have the freedom to act in ways that they believe will enhance the performance of colleagues and the organization. To achieve this trifecta, and to truly engage people, our research and experience suggest that senior leaders and direct managers must take four steps:

INFORM employees about business operations and challenges, and clearly show how those factors link to employees' day-to-day responsibilities.

Gather **INPUT** from employees via personal contact and organizational channels, and acknowledge and appropriately act on their ideas and contributions.

Create opportunities and freedom for colleagues to **COLLABORATE** on important issues.

Give employees **THE AUTHORITY** to improve
operations, reduce costs, and assist customers—on
their jobs and through special projects.

The remainder of this chapter is organized around these four concepts.

Inform Employees for Improved Performance

During college, Honeywell CEO Dave Cote spent two-and-a-half years as an hourly employee on a manufacturing floor. "I was not a genius or a miracle worker, but in general I thought I did a good job," he recalls. "But I was basically clueless about the company and what we were trying to do." Perhaps if he had been given the big picture and understood what his group or department was trying to accomplish, he would have done some things differently. Nonetheless, this experience from his youth has colored Cote's current management philosophy:

> The company at the time was trying to get us focused on quality, and they put up a big quality board in all the aisles. No one took it seriously. No one explained it. I remember looking at it during my break trying to figure it out . . . I wasn't a simpleton. My foreman did not understand it either. I thought, "If I ever get anywhere, this is the kind of stuff I will remember." Communication has to be straightforward. It must relate to everyone on the floor so they get why it is important . . . today, in conversations I have with people [about how] to touch 125,000 employees, I say, "How do we convey this in a way that makes sense to them?"

Informing employees to help improve their individual performance comes down to three steps for the organization and individual managers.

First, make people "business literate"—explaining in some detail how the organization and their unit operate and make money, and how competitors and external challenges affect the financial situation. Second, give employees a "line of sight" from the work they do every day to the organization's larger goals and mission. Third, provide workers at all levels with the latest business data to help them better serve customers, improve operations, and make decisions day by day.

The point is not to flood employees with reams of information, but rather to show a fundamental respect for people's judgment, time, and savvy. When relevant information is shared in a straightforward manner, most people will understand it, use it as it's intended, and appropriately integrate it into their work. Informing employees in these ways should be a part of every company's standard operating procedures, not something that occurs only during periods of change or at annual meetings.

Collectively, employees make millions of decisions each day that affect the business, from how they prioritize their tasks, to how carefully they review a document, to how much time they spend with a disgruntled customer. If they continually make those decisions in an information vacuum, they might not only make poor choices, but could make bad situations even worse. Giving employees enough context to connect their daily decisions and behaviors to the organization's big picture helps ensure that their choices and actions are as well thought out as possible and that their actions advance the organization's objective in the smartest manner possible.

CREATE A BUSINESS-LITERATE WORKFORCE

The purpose of business literacy—essentially, knowledge of the organization's inner workings as well as the marketplace in which the company operates—is not to endow everyone with a mini-MBA, but to give employees at all levels sufficient context to understand how their decisions and behaviors make a difference to the organization, and to provide a common language and vision to work effectively with their colleagues.

The bigger the organization and the wider its geographic reach and span of operations, the easier it is for employees to lose sight of how their individual actions fit with others to achieve a broader goal. The Winchester Mystery House in San Jose, California, provides a stark metaphor for what can happen without a clear vision of the bigger picture. The house that Sarah Winchester, the Winchester Rifle heiress, built in the late 1800s is an architectural marvel, with its exquisite designs and then-modern amenities, including elevators. However, the house was built without a master plan, and because of this it has major architectural gaffes, such as stairwells that go nowhere and doors that open up to walls.

Avoiding such mistakes for any company requires providing employees with an overview that includes basic financial and operational information. Partly, this is about developing the rational side of engagement—helping people better understand the *what* and *why* of their jobs so they can make more educated choices about how to spend time and focus energy. But business knowledge also supports the emotional side of engagement because, once informed, employees are more likely to feel connected and have a greater sense of purpose in their work. In short, people who grasp how their day-to-day activities fit into and affect the operations of the whole organization are more likely to put forth discretionary effort to help the company achieve that mission.

As CEO of Honeywell, one of Dave Cote's goals has been to demystify business processes to avoid the confusion and apathy he experienced as a young worker. In the following excerpt from a recent letter to employees, he tried to do that by explaining some business basics and describing how the company is addressing pressing issues. Note his focus on *why* these things are important:

> Cash is a major indicator of how well we are executing operationally, and it allows us to add to our company's value through acquisitions, dividends, and share repurchases. Working capital—a key driver of cash—is a reflection of how well we run our business. Money that is tied up in working capital is *not* available to help us grow or return value to shareowners. We have planned for working capital improvements to deliver about $300 million in cash this year, so there is much we need to do. Dave Anderson, Honeywell senior vice president and chief financial officer, and his team of CFOs are meeting monthly to review free cash flow and working capital performance, and they are driving a series of actions to improve how we're doing across the board. Reducing working capital is *everyone's* job. We need to identify and fix breakdowns in our operations that increase cycle time and inventory, or that hurt accounts receivable and payable. Improving our working capital performance requires accountability and discipline across a series of processes—understanding our customers, producing accurate goods and invoices, and having strong collections. This is a big deal, and we need everyone to focus on it.

Since 2002, Cote has also given quarterly, company-wide broadcasts. He uses these messages to emphasize what's important about the company's current state. "I want everyone to view me as consistent and transparent so they do not have to figure out my real agenda," he says. After each broadcast, Honeywell measures feedback from employees who tuned in. Some recent data reveal the broadcasts' power: 83 percent of some 5,000 employees who responded to the survey in January 2008 said they had an "improved understanding of the company's overall direction and were clear on what they need to do to contribute."

At a Honeywell sales office in Lubbock, Texas, forty-nine-year-old administrative assistant Marcia Kiser—who hails from a farming and ranching background and has a degree in marketing—credits the additional business knowledge she gleans from her direct bosses for improving her ongoing efforts to collect overdue invoices, even though it's not her primary responsibility.

> My management has always called me in and shown me how the pieces fit together . . . because I have a good understanding of the financial picture of how we operate, I know how a sale actually flows through the company, or how it will impact over-all revenue. That is a huge benefit for me because it provides a deeper understanding.

One month, when her branch had a big push to reduce outstanding receivables, Kiser understood why: "Anything outstanding costs us money because we carry that money and we are financing it." In just thirty days, Kiser collected more than $750,000 from customers. What's more, she shares her knowledge with other administrators in the branch, who in turn make their own collection calls. Honeywell has appropriately rewarded Kiser's efforts, as we shall see in the next chapter.

When employees understand the company—its history, its

operations, its breadth of offerings—they can more fully service and represent the brand, not just a niche product or service. A star salesperson at EMC, Kyle Leciejewski exceeded his 2007 sales quota by 190 percent, bringing in $5.5 million in revenue that year. When asked what makes him so successful, he explained:

> Without a doubt, I know the company as a whole. You do not win deals by talking about "speed and feed" . . . you have to sell the company. The way I beat the competition is to tell EMC's story, how we were formed, why we went public, and when. There is a whole pitch I have that differentiates EMC . . . you have to know the company story to do your job effectively.

REI store manager Rachel Ligtenberg offers a manager's perspective on the value of creating a business-literate workforce. Each January, Ligtenberg distributes her business plan—a list of store goals and priorities—to her 400-plus member staff. "The more informed every staff member is, the more passionate they are to contribute to our success," she says. Respect leads to better behaviors, which in turn contribute to better financial performance. Recall that in the seven years since Ligtenberg took over the Seattle store, profits have increased more than 70 percent.

Share Fresh Data and Daily Details

If business literacy sets the larger context, sharing daily data and details gives employees a steady flow of information that is, by its nature, constantly in flux. Both types of information help employees make better daily decisions, but the latter even more so.

Considering how easy it is to inundate people with data today, the challenge for organizations is to give employees appropriate information they can easily access, sort, and use when it's most important.

When Campbell employees were asked what they wanted from an internal company-wide website, the number one response was the ability to find accurate information easily, be it from the latest performance review documents or from lists of product information. Campbell responded in kind. Says head of HR Nancy Reardon, "Part of feeling engaged is feeling informed, and our website provides people with information to do their job, whether it's about the company, about a new SAP implementation, how we are changing expense accounts, or launching new low-sodium soups." Today, the site also lets employees preview new ads, track the company's stock, and follow industry trends.

At Honeywell's Muskegon plant, manager David Price began updating shop floor workers daily on where the plant stood regarding monthly production goals:

> We used to update workers at the end of every week and month; now workers know at the end of the shift where they and the plant stand in terms of being on track to reach goals. If you were supposed to fill fifty cases in an hour, you will know if you only filled forty. The actual data is posted on the factory floor . . . we are trying to get everyone to make little improvements every day; to do that, we have to share information with all employees so they can do the right thing and initiate improvements.

Exposing line workers to the same data that managers routinely review has helped the plant improve on-time delivery rates. In the

same vein, informing line workers about daily operational details—
not necessarily just the numbers—helps improve customer
service.

As we'll discuss in the next chapter, when Gamal Aziz became
president of MGM Grand, one of his goals was to create a workforce
that delivered the best possible customer experience. Aziz understood
that lack of information hindered employees' ability to deliver the
superior level of guest services that his renovated hotel and casino
would demand.

As noted earlier, Aziz and his staff put in place the daily Pre-Shift
meeting to share operational information with the entire workforce.
Each day, hourly workers' shifts begin with this ten-minute
departmental gathering. At each Pre-Shift, a supervisor reviews a
summary of everything happening at the hotel on that particular
day, from the number of occupied rooms and special groups visiting
the hotel to the start and stop times for shows and events. Employees
are also alerted to the visits of any VIP guests. At the Pre-Shift
meeting we attended, twenty tuxedo-clad dealers listened as their
supervisor told them the hotel was at 100 percent capacity and
1,700 employees from Prudential Japan were checking in that day
with their families, including some 500 children. The message to
dealers? Be prepared to suggest kid-friendly places at the hotel that
guests can visit, such as the lion habitat, the arcade, or the pool.
Armed with this and other daily details, employees throughout the
organization were poised to better help guests enjoy their stay,
regardless of their specific job.

Employees become more engaged when they take an interest in
what they are making or selling, but first they must be informed.
In-person sessions like the Pre-Shift meeting ensure that they are.
Most MGM Grand workers do not have regular access to computers,
and many would likely miss the same information if it were just

posted on a bulletin board or sent via e-mail. For example, if waiters and chefs at all of MGM Grand's restaurants know the Elton John concert will end at 10:30 p.m., they better prepare for a sudden rush of late-night diners. President Aziz told us the first thing he does each morning is read the daily Pre-Shift e-mail. "Even I need to know what's going on!" he says.

The Pre-Shift is a deceptively simple tactic. To make it succeed, senior leaders must allow a high degree of hotel information to be made public to the workforce. And, they must put short-term performance in the context of long-term results so people don't feel micromanaged. Departments must supply updated information on a daily basis to the communications department, which in turn must have company-wide information ready to disseminate first thing each morning. The Pre-Shift tactic also requires supervisors to be consistently present and visible to their staff, and it requires employees to show up on time for the meetings. No doubt, the daily Pre-Shift approach has helped MGM Grand earn its fifty-four Four- and Five-Star Diamond awards from AAA.

Create Line-of-Sight Understanding

Line of sight refers to an individual's ability to directly connect his or her daily tasks with the broader objectives of the unit, division, or even the corporation itself. The clearer the line of sight, the better the employee sees the connection between what he does and how the company performs. He better understands the right way to approach a task: how much time to give it, and so on. In turn, the employee contributes valuable results, which further increases his emotional connection to the organization. It becomes another example of the virtuous circle of activity and engagement: the more closely we understand our organization rationally, the more valuable our contributions; and the more valuable our contributions, the more emotionally connected we feel, so the more discretionary effort we are willing to give.

Our research underscores this critical connection between line of sight and engagement. As specified in chapter 1 (Exhibit C), among the global respondents to our *Global Workforce Study,* 88 percent of the engaged employees believed they could have a positive impact on quality, and 85 percent believed they could influence customer service. By contrast, a mere 38 percent of the disengaged employees thought they could positively impact quality, and only 42 percent believed they could influence customer service. This line-of-sight understanding is required to move people to act. Drawing a clear line from an employee's day-to-day responsibilities to quality, the customer experience, and overall financial results will improve employees' understanding and enable them to make the right decisions and do the right things to add value to the company every day.

Creating these connections is easier in some jobs than in others. It's pretty clear that employees who deal directly with customers have an impact on the customer experience. But even here, there are important nuances. Consider the actions of an engaged customer service representative at a bank who helps a customer whose wallet and credit cards were stolen. She proactively asks about the customer's ATM card and even offers to get a replacement driver's license from the local department of motor vehicles. The bank representative doesn't wait for the customer to ask when new cards will be mailed or how the account will be monitored, but volunteers that information and offers other useful tips for protecting against identity theft. This employee understands the difference between just satisfying a customer and ensuring a customer's loyalty. A loyal customer is more likely to stay with the bank and use additional services from the bank than a satisfied customer. Engaged workers are intent on enhancing loyalty because, in part, they understand the financial impact, in terms of sustained and increased business.

A more complicated example of line of sight is a grocery store manager's decision about the number of cashiers to employ at various points throughout the day. First, the manager has to balance the need for enough cashiers to eliminate long lines for customers with the cost of scheduling additional cashiers. The informed manager understands the interplay between wait time on the checkout line, customer satisfaction, repeat business, operating costs, and profitability. Armed with this information, she can decide to add a cashier to the morning shift to reduce wait times and minimize the risk of customers defecting to another store. In addition, she realizes she can cut back a cashier from the evening shift because customer impatience is less of an issue at that time of day. Her knowledge of all the business factors that come into play results in a decision that reduces the company's costs without adversely impacting customer loyalty.

Line of sight can be drawn even for jobs that seem very far removed from the customer. At North Shore–LIJ Carol Battaglia is the director of benefit operations for the Human Resources Service Center. Battaglia's job is essentially a backroom role—she's not performing heart surgery or taking patients' temperatures—and for many years she never considered how her daily administrative duties on behalf of hospital workers' own insurance needs might affect patient care. Then, one of the courses she took at North Shore–LIJ's Center for Learning and Innovation (CLI) taught her otherwise. Battaglia and her classmates were briefed about the hospitals' routines and procedures, including insights into how and when nurses do their jobs. Unlike most office workers, nurses cannot simply pick up a phone or check e-mail whenever they feel like it; instead, they get brief breaks to catch their breath.

That understanding was like a lightbulb that helped change how Battaglia and her HR colleagues went about their jobs, including how they handled personnel calls that came into the HR department each day. Battaglia came to realize that an inquiry from a nurse on break that went unanswered by HR for an unacceptable period of time could put a debilitating crimp in the nurse's mood. Says Battaglia:

> Say a nurse makes a call to us on her fifteen-minute break to say that she has a problem with her benefits, but she can't get through to talk to anyone. What if she gets frustrated and when she goes back to work isn't as friendly to the patient as she could be? For years I did not realize how, for example, not answering my phone could impact a patient in another building. I am off-site, and it was helpful for me to see what the doctors and nurses are up against every day.

Once she "got it," Battaglia helped improve the way the HR department responded to employee inquiries. Today, a dedicated HR Service Center includes a single HR phone number that all North Shore–LIJ employees can call with pay- and benefit-related questions. A customized, automated service directs them to the right department, or lets them leave a voice message or input their phone number to get an automatic callback. Battaglia puts one staffer in charge of answering employee calls every day, and HR staffers are expected to get back to employees as soon as possible, not simply when it is convenient for them.

This example makes two significant points. First, Battaglia was taught, in detail, how doctors and nurses deliver patient care, and the new knowledge spurred her to fix inefficient HR procedures. Second, as an individual employee, Battaglia told us that she feels more involved in the organization because she now understands how her back-office work can actually affect patients, as well as her internal customers. Note also that, in both cases, what compelled Battaglia was the human dynamic. Ultimately, empathy for the needs and circumstances of others—colleagues, patients, customers—is what made the difference. Battaglia is not alone. Eighty-five percent of North Shore–LIJ employees feel they, too, have a good line of sight as to how their jobs contribute to the organization as a whole, according to internal surveys.

Line of sight can be like a road with loops, turns, and forks. Leaders need to give employees information and tools so they understand which path to take to gain the optimal result for the company.

Gather Employee Input to Leverage Experience and Foster Creative Problem Solving

Participation engages hearts and minds. Passive observation keeps people on the sidelines. Engaging organizations give people opportunities, not just orders, and employee input can be encouraged with an invitation. You and your organization can provide avenues for people to share opinions, ideas, improvements, even frustrations. As long as the input gathered is acted on or, at the very least, acknowledged, efforts to solicit it will feel genuine.

In this section we'll explore two primary ways your organization can effectively encourage and harvest employees' input: informal boss-employee dialogue and formal feedback instruments.

Boss-Employee Dialogues

Few things are more disengaging than a boss who doesn't listen. Engaging leaders and managers invite and really hear people's feedback. Even if employee ideas are not adopted, people must believe they were heard and their ideas were considered. At Honeywell, three levels of managers use formal and informal tactics to solicit ideas.

First, CEO Dave Cote explains his efforts to involve his executive team in high-level decision making:

> Make sure you're willing to listen, but being willing to listen does not mean you always have to agree. There is a big difference, and someone does not have to agree to prove they were listening. If a decision needs to get made, I make it, and if it goes against what two or three other people suggested, I try to take the time to explain the rationale so they do not feel they were just wrong and that I was not listening. I try to convey, "Here is why I am making the decision that I am, and what I am weighing or willing to risk given the goal." I try to explain because it reinforces the listening . . . I don't want them leaving the room saying it is not worth bringing new ideas to me because I shoot everything down. I explain my thought process. If they see me doing it, I think there will be a greater chance that they will do it, too. Let me put it this way: If I do not act that way, then I know they won't do it. But by acting that way, there is a greater chance that they will.

Cote's former direct report, Nance Dicciani (who retired from Honeywell in 2008), ran Honeywell's Specialty Materials unit and took her own approach with her unit's 10,000 workers. About every two months she held Coffee with Nance, an informal session with employees at their local offices. Dicciani would speak for a few minutes about the state of the business and then answer questions. She also held what she called Skip-Level box lunches, gathering around a table with up to two dozen employees who were all a few levels below her, but without their direct managers present. Dicciani elaborates:

> These are very well received. It puts me in touch with the people in the organization in a way I could not otherwise be. They ask me questions and talk about what's on their minds. We talk about what's going right as well as wrong. And we talk about how their jobs are important to the future of the organization, and it just makes them feel a whole lot more connected . . . But it doesn't work unless I really listen to what people say and acknowledge it. And if there are follow-up items, you do in fact have to follow up. I think people want to know, and feel, that they are being listened to, so the discussion has to be genuine.

At the Muskegon, Michigan, chemical-solvent plant, manager David Price routinely walks the shop floor or invites workers into his office and asks them to suggest ways that he, as well as the plant, can do better. "Not everyone is comfortable giving me honest feedback, but when they do, I have to have a thick skin and really listen to them," says Price. A snowball effect ensues. Once employees know Price is receptive to new ideas, they are more likely to volunteer them. Recently, some workers were packaging a large, fragile customer order into boxes one at a time, but because the process was taking too long, they risked missing a deadline. Rather than shrug and keep his head down, one worker voluntarily suggested they move the whole operation to a larger production room where there was more space to reconfigure the machines. They did, and cut production time by almost one-third, making the deadline.

Another Engaging Eight organization, McKesson, formalized the process of gathering input by "encouraging, almost to the point of insisting," that the company's top 350 managers ask members of their teams how they could improve as part of their own performance development. With each boss asking at least ten people to offer feedback, thousands of employees get an invitation to offer ideas. "This injects an amount of humility that hierarchical structures usually do not support," says Paul Kirincic, executive VP of human resources. "Employees feel valued because they are being asked for input." While such efforts must be carefully designed and positioned, they provide an extremely efficient and comprehensive way to connect employees with the work of continually improving the organization.

Just knowing they have opportunities to voice opinions—even frustrations usually reserved for hushed gossip sessions behind closed doors—can make people feel valued, more engaged, and more likely to volunteer performance-enhancing ideas.

FORMAL FEEDBACK INSTRUMENTS

Whether it's a physical suggestion box in the lunch room, an online idea blog, or a virtual innovation jam, an organization should establish at least one formal, readily available, easily accessible vehicle for employee input. This conveys that the organization is always interested in anything employees have to offer, at any time. The best ideas for enhancing business will come from within the business—not from a group of disconnected developers working in an ivory tower. And they can come at any time. As Vijay Govindarajan, director of global leadership at the Tuck School of Business at Dartmouth, believes: the CEO should be listening to the voices of the people on the ground who are able to see the future. Govindarajan makes it clear that the CEO's responsibility is to encourage lots of ideas, and then spot the ones that will help the company achieve its mission.

Consider the well-publicized virtual innovation jam that IBM CEO Sam Palmisano hosted. As reported on IBM's corporate website, he invited all 335,000 IBMers to participate in an electronic brainstorming session to develop ideas that would move the company forward. The jam lasted for three days and generated 37,000 comments from 53,000 employees. IBM has committed $100 million to develop these ideas and is now taking steps to involve employees in prioritizing the ideas based on greatest market and social impact. More important, IBM has turned its jam concept into an ongoing approach to collecting ideas, and the new ThinkPlace program gives anyone in the company an opportunity to suggest ideas, comment on them, support them, or refine them.

Other companies like Infosys and Research in Motion (the BlackBerry people) introduced formal programs to hear the voice of employees directly. Infosys's approach is to select a small group of "next generation" employees and invite them to participate in senior management meetings alongside company executives. Research in Motion invites people to visioning sessions each month to hear their ideas for new research and future goals.

Create Opportunities for Collegial Collaboration

Another facet of involvement entails the degree to which and ways that employees are involved with each other—working on projects, solving problems, serving customers. Throughout our interviews with engaged employees and engaging managers, we heard reference to how important it was for them to work well with colleagues to achieve both individual and company goals. Without the sense of community that comes from interacting with peers, it is tougher to be involved in your organization's operations, and tougher to feel engaged.

When employees talk about collaboration, they aren't just referring to the teamwork that's part of virtually every job today, but also involvement in projects outside their regular responsibilities. Opportunities to collaborate—or rather, an environment that makes it easy to work with other people—come about via a mix of formal company procedures and the informal aspects of corporate culture.

Interdepartmental work groups and special-project teams are excellent opportunities to capture and apply employee contributions, and for many organizations the only way to fulfill the mission. At Novartis, scientific advancement is critical to the pharmaceutical company's ability to meet patients' needs. Collaboration and diversity of ideas is a prerequisite for product innovation.

"Health care is highly complex and highly regulated," says Kamran Tavangar, who has been with Novartis in various global jobs since 1991, most recently as head of strategic global marketing for Novartis Vaccines. "There's a lot riding on our product—mainly human life—that we need to be cognizant about, so we need the expert opinion of a variety of people to work in harmony toward a goal. We need people with strong individual competencies in their areas of responsibility, who are also able to work with other highly capable individuals, to discuss how the whole thing needs to come together toward a winning goal." Tavangar adds that working well together requires everyone involved to be a good listener, to be open to new ideas, and to be able to articulate their points and concerns in a concise, positive, and constructive fashion.

In her post as global head of Novartis's Clinical Development Operations in Basel, Nora Dyer's job was to form and manage productive teams. Now head of drug regulatory affairs in Europe, Dyer describes the role collaboration plays in meeting objectives, and touches on the importance of informing team members as well as granting them autonomy:

> To get anything done you must get teams across a range of disciplines. Projects like drug development are by nature cross-functional, and you can't get anything done without others. Individuals cannot have the same level of success unless they are with a team. It is not by serendipity that people work together. We have structures in place to facilitate collaboration. For me, my biggest success has been working with a very strong team of highly skilled, empowered individuals. As their leader, I need to step back, look at the big picture, and identify key issues. To be most effective, you need to get the team's buy-in—why are we doing what we are doing—you can't just tell people to do things. People need to understand why they are doing something and what the benefits and measurements will be. Giving the team freedom to come up with new ideas and how to do things differently is always energizing. I do not micromanage. I lead in a way that opens the door for others' ideas.

Collaboration is a cultural mind-set at companies such as Novartis, but it's not always easy, especially when organizations are dispersed geographically and defined by line function. Successful collaboration requires individual outreach and discretionary effort: each individual must be willing to pick up the phone and participate in a dialogue or project when a colleague from another department, city, or country calls for assistance. Novartis's Tom Hughes says, "We are an incredibly collaborative organization. On any given day you have 4,000 collaborators, any of whom you can make a business call to and who will gladly help you."

Honeywell also tries to make interdepartmental collaboration an intrinsic way of doing business. Mike Bennett, a vice president of communications in the Specialty Materials business unit, points out that the ability "to quickly and easily form work teams for projects" is unusually easy at Honeywell, and entrenched in the company's culture. At Bennett's former employer, he says he had to ask a colleague's supervisor to involve people on a project, and people were often suspicious of why you wanted to work with them. "Here you just identify who you want to work with and call them. I am always amazed at how readily they come together to form a team. People from different departments work together not because they are told to do so, but because they understand the power of doing so."

In Honeywell's HR department, Vice President Mary Anne Robinson formed a team to help create the company's new HR processes. Says Robinson, "It's a way to let people from all over the world contribute via giving their opinion about HR policies; just an hour or two of someone's time a month is not too burdensome, and it's nice to be asked to participate in a project."

One way to encourage employees to proactively and voluntarily participate is to provide opportunities for people from different departments and offices to meet each other before they even need to work together. Time and time again, employees told us that when they could put a face with an e-mail message or voice on the other end of the phone, they were more likely to help. At Campbell, new employees' bosses help them identify and arrange informational meetings with people with whom they may have to interact to do their jobs. As part of his Meet-and-Greet, Anthony Sanzio, group director of corporate and brand communications, met with twenty-five to thirty people over the course of two months. "Everyone made time. Each time I met with someone, I asked, 'Who else should I meet?' They gave me additional names, people I would have to call for certain subjects. It was helpful when I had to call people especially under deadline because we had already had a face-to-face meeting and they already knew who I was and my role."

Sanzio's Campbell colleague Judy Freedman, says internal networking through in-house organizations, like the Women of Campbell Network, has helped her diversify her involvement. "I have colleagues I am friendly with in finance and audit and other areas. I know I can call on them when I have a business question or if I need a project to get funded."

Collaboration can also happen virtually. EMC created an internal, online tool it calls EMC.ONE that lets employees at all levels of the organization, located anywhere, share ideas. In the four months since EMC created this internal social networking site, more than 2,700 employees have contributed ideas to it, and about 3,000 more peruse it. Participants blog and collaborate on product development, and they compare best practices—on a global scale and in multiple languages. Employees share information on competitors and views from prospective customers that can be used to help salespeople in the field. The nature of the social networking beast gives everyone equal opportunity to contribute. Says EMC's Polly Pearson:

> Those who contribute the most meaningful content become the most powerful, regardless of tenure, title, geographic location, or other considerations. What are the employees getting

from using the social network? Connection, respect, interesting conversations, recognition, skill development, empowerment, a sense of belonging, and proof that what they do matters. Within the social network, they get to be a part of something that feels big and important and yet still personal. What does EMC get? Connections that otherwise would never have happened that ignite great ideas and great action. Global unity. A means to spread and further inculcate its culture. More passion and commitment from its people.

EMC's analysis of its own employee surveys proves how important collaboration is to its workers. Consider these two factors that EMC employees say significantly affect their engagement and satisfaction: (1) the level of enjoyment that an employee gets working with others and (2) the cooperative relationships an employee has with and across work groups. In these areas, EMC employees report highly favorable scores: 91 percent of EMC's employees say the people in their work group cooperate to get work done; 88 percent say their work group cooperates with other work groups to achieve business goals; and 93 percent enjoy working with their coworkers.

Indeed, how we feel about the people we work *with*—not just the people we work *for*—has tremendous impact on our ability to be involved, to feel engaged, and thus on overall performance. EMC CEO Joe Tucci is emphatic on this point:

> I do not care how talented you are, if you cannot work as part of a team, you cannot reach ultimate success. By yourself you can only accomplish so much. But with a passionate team that wants to work together, you can accomplish anything in life. I have taken very talented smart people who did not play on a team and shown them the door.

Freedom to Act

Both teams and individuals benefit from a degree of independence, or freedom from management interference, to make decisions and act on them in the best interests of the organization. This feeling of autonomy, versus feeling hamstrung, manifests itself in one's ability to make or shape decisions and drives engagement. Unfortunately, many leaders look at autonomy and see a cousin of anarchy. Therefore, they are less inclined to give people room to maneuver and more likely to focus on controls and consistency. While this may not be intended to hold people back, such intense focus can do just that.

Consider what can happen when management lets go. In 2004, McKesson bought Moore Medical, a small supplier of health care products for physicians' offices, EMF agencies, and fire rescue squads. Within six months of the acquisition, ten of Moore's top eleven executives left, including the CEO. Almost overnight, Moore's middle managers found themselves free from the hierarchy and layers of approval that shackled them in the past. At the same time, they were beholden to mandatory performance metrics imposed by their new, publicly held parent company. Without a thick layer of micromanagers, Moore's 300 employees suddenly found themselves, well, free to act. "The McKesson acquisition unleashed us!" says Todd Baldanzi, then vice president of Moore Medical. He describes the journey:

> Before the acquisition, progress was slow. So no matter if someone had a great idea, structurally it was not the culture to bring it forward. We stopped taking chances and risks, and usually just stayed in our offices. Once we had been acquired and once the management team was not there, layers of

middle management got the opportunity to step up and show what we could do. It was a nice opportunity for people at a point in their careers when they were ready to take on more responsibility. There was a strong focus on hitting our numbers, and we knew the sum of our performance was measured on profitability. It felt very natural to work together to figure it out and get it done. Once we got rid of roadblocks and bureaucracy, I was freed to walk down to someone's office and say, "Here is a way to make more money. Let's try it." We would gather in a room and come up with incremental plans to sell more products and increase margins. Someone might say, "Here is a way to save $20,000, mind if I take the lead on it?" Give a group of people more then they can handle, they do more than you expect. It has been the most rewarding experience.

    . . . You have to have some rules to run a multimillion-dollar company, but you cannot be so bureaucratic that you slow speed and innovation and the ability to make quick decisions. We would try out some ideas in small pilots before we asked permission. If they demonstrated success, then we got approval to do it on a larger scale.

McKesson's acquisition of Moore Medical paid for itself in less than four years. Today, Moore's sales are up and the company is profitable.

Moore's tale demonstrates not only what can be achieved with effective collaboration, but the discretionary effort that people will put forth when they have an appropriate amount of autonomy to act in ways that improve the business. When bosses give some independence to those on the front lines—especially those dealing with customer concerns—work can become a far more rewarding experience. But when people feel compelled to rely on company-provided scripts, for example, or canned responses, it limits their potential to solve problems creatively.

Novartis also recognizes that bureaucracy is an enemy of autonomy. In a global survey of the top 350 executives at Novartis, people expressed a desire for greater "simplicity," meaning less bureaucracy. While not a complete surprise to Novartis's management—international pharmaceuticals is a complicated business—it reacted to what the workforce said it needed. "We told the workforce that we heard them and wanted to create simpler processes," says Dr. Juergen Brokatzky-Geiger, who heads global HR. Each division was asked to create a formal action plan to simplify processes, such as reducing the number of approval levels for capital improvement requests. "We are a big complex company and have a lot of elements that people can perceive as limiting their freedom, so the challenge for us is how to take a big organization and make it feel small." This was especially important for Novartis's scientists, one of its most valued employee groups whose creativity and enthusiasm would be seriously undermined by complicated and time-consuming organizational procedures that did not relate to the science at hand.

Increased autonomy does not imply absolute freedom without boundaries and accountability. The degree of autonomy provided at each job level should be enough to make people feel in control and able to contribute to the organization, but not so much that one person's or one group's acts can sabotage the whole. A simple example is an airline's customer service representative who has the freedom to address business travelers' complaints in ways she feels are appropriate, but not beyond, say, a cost of $500 per passenger. She can't, for example, give a family of four round-trip tickets to Hawaii, but she can, without seeking permission from a superior or getting into trouble, opt to upgrade a disgruntled passenger to first class on a future trip. Or, turn on a movie for the passengers of a flight that's been delayed on the ground for three hours.

Even with autonomy, people must still be held accountable for their actions. This is a tough line to define, no doubt. Novartis's CEO, Dr. Daniel Vasella, speaks about the relationship between engagement, autonomy, and accountability:

> From the simplest to the most complex jobs, people want to feel in control of their destiny, that they can shape it. It's much easier to engage them if they feel they are controlled more from the inside than the outside. But it's a fine line, they have to come back and tell you what they achieved. Here, I think, the company's values play a very important role in that they define how people achieve; the values act as boundaries. If we are clear about values and how we expect people to behave, then you do not need too many controls because you have moral boundaries.

His attitude helps create legions of employees who deliver results. As you will recall, 80 percent of Novartis's top global leaders are characterized as very engaged. Says Kamran Tavangar, head of strategic global marketing and a previous head of investor relations in the United States:

> One characteristic of Daniel Vasella is his ability to get more out of you than you thought possible from yourself. When you are entrusted with responsibility, you are personally not satisfied with anything less than world class because your role models do not accept anything less. The successful Novartis

managers are self-starters; they take on a challenge with plea-
sure. I never worried about how many hours it took me to get
something done. I worried about what I got done . . . Novartis
gave me the ability to operate as a manager with some leeway
as to what makes sense toward achieving maximum impact.

One result of Tavangar's engagement can be seen in how he
increased the degree of North American investment and confidence
in the Swiss company. When Tavangar became head of U.S. investor
relations in 2000, ADRs—American depositary receipts, which
represent dollar-denominated ownership of shares in a foreign
company traded in U.S. financial markets—traded at about 150,000
shares a day. Novartis's goal was to hit 1 million ADRs traded daily.
With freedom to solve the problem as he saw fit and with strong
management support, Tavangar first educated himself about the
U.S. investor marketplace, spending almost two years talking with
sell-side and buy-side analysts, hedge funds managers, and investors
about what they needed to feel comfortable investing in foreign
stocks. "I learned that the key thing the investment community
wanted was confidence that they could quickly and reliably reach
someone who knew the details of the business," he says. He delivered
by getting Novartis's senior management in front of U.S. investors
in a timely fashion to answer questions and by setting up meetings
with key investors immediately after quarterly earnings statements
were released. He also created a department dedicated to answering
investors' calls quickly.

In the financial world, they don't want surprises. Of course,
positive surprises are readily accepted but have a half-life
measurable in days, while the life of a negative surprise can

be years . . . so you have to make sure negative news is put into context as soon as possible. When the FDA rejected one of our products to everyone's surprise, I was up in Boston with Fidelity within the week to talk to them; the mere fact that I was willing to sit in front of them at a time of this major surprise was taken very positively and communicated that we were a company that did not run away from issues. That transparency and clarity was what they wanted, and the fact that I could also discuss it with them in both pharmaceutical and financial terms was also something they could really appreciate. Because we also worked with them systematically over time— explaining the guts of the organization—they knew what the inherent value of the company was.

By the time Tavangar left the job in 2004 to lead oncology in Australia and New Zealand, his team had reached Novartis's goal: almost 1 million Novartis shares traded a day, and the ADRs as a percentage of total shares approached 15 percent. Six years after listing on the New York Stock Exchange, Novartis was the fifth most widely held ADR on the NYSE.

Autonomy to act, to make decisions, and to solve problems is a universal value for employees who produce results for Honeywell. At Honeywell's Technology Solutions Lab in India—which has been named one of the top ten Best Places to Work in India and maintains a retention rate double that of other India-based technology organizations—the on-site managing director, Krishna Mikkilineni, tells team leaders to feel like they are running their own company, and that destiny is in their hands. He tells these leaders that he expects them to act in an entrepreneurial way, and that they don't need permission for every decision or have to wait for someone to tell them what to do. "When people take more ownership for their actions, there is a sense that they will do what needs to be done to get the right results. That atmosphere helps ensure that our company is successful," says Mikkilineni.

He also gives them freedom to visit customers and Honeywell operations in other regions, and return with new ideas to improve their own operations. These self-initiated outings further educate employees about the products they sell because they see firsthand how a client is actually using them. Says Mikkilineni:

> Having that freedom, that mandate to be able to explore the environment around them and bring additional opportunities to the company is something that may be unique compared to other India-based companies. Employees start to perceive the product in a bigger sense, and making the context bigger for people is very important . . . Workers like to have their talents leveraged . . . when employers ask employees to create something beyond just their job description, people feel like someone really valued them as a whole being rather than just a good worker. People do not want to feel they are being straitjacketed by their jobs. They want freedom to do more than just their job description so they can learn, and that is a big deal to people; they think, "Hey, someone is looking for us to contribute as a 'full person' rather than just getting some part of us."

There is no right degree of autonomy to endow. Much depends on the individuals involved, their skill level, and what's at stake. Again, McKesson's Todd Baldanzi recalled how Moore Medical's employees felt stifled when management was too directive. That said, autonomy does not mean management should give employees complete flexibility either. When freedom is coupled with moral and financial boundaries as well as accountability, we believe employees will be more likely than not to take initiative that drives results.

In Closing: The Involved Employee

"I'm treated as an equal voice in the implementation team, that's a motivating factor for me." Damon Wolters is reflecting on why he feels engaged at the Honeywell plant managed by David Price in Muskegon, Michigan. A chemical operator at the plant for more than nine years, Wolters's intellectual and emotional connections were not always so deep.

Before Price took over, Wolters was among many shop floor workers who felt frustrated and disconnected from their work. Rather than stew, Wolters—a former Air Force munitions expert— volunteered to work with the plant's managers as they rolled out the new Honeywell Operating System, the work approach created by Honeywell CEO Dave Cote and his executive team. Wolters's new role came with no additional salary or title change, but he explains in his own words how his increased involvement in plant processes has spurred his engagement level:

> In the past, people didn't always feel part of the solution, but feared they would be pointed out as part of the problem. The solutions were left to "experts," and people like me were just here to execute. My job was to punch the clock and go home.
>
> So when a pilot team from Corporate came to the plant to help introduce the concept of HOS and what it meant, I was one of the first who volunteered to take time off from my regular job to spend time with the team and work on some of the

technical changes. I pursued the new role out of curiosity and frustration. I wanted to protect my interests—the job and what my job entails—and I wanted my job to make sense. It was an exciting time for me.

Before I took the role I was quite uneasy about management's intentions. Now, a layer of management is no longer there, and I work directly with the plant manager. David and I spend a lot of time talking about what needs to happen to implement new processes and sustain them. He continues to spend a lot of time explaining where he wants to take us and why. I think what I contribute is probably just a reminder to the management team to keep things simple, and that more complex is not always best . . . I think I have brought a sensibility to keep processes clean and neat.

I came off the shop floor and was given a certain amount of dignity and credibility from the plant manager, and that's very motivating for me. What he demonstrates to me on an individual level is that he believes in me, that he thinks I have good ideas and feels confident in my involvement and ability to contribute to our improvement initiatives. For the past five months I have not spent my time making any saleable goods, but contributing my ideas. Price is investing in my perspective, which is a shop floor perspective.

Wolters's experience touches on the themes that define and drive employee involvement and contribute to engagement. He's become more informed about the business, and he understands why the plant's managers are making certain changes. At the same time, his input is invited and considered as changes are made. The temporary role and management's openness to his ideas give Wolters a sense of independence and freedom from structure, a feeling that will likely remain when and if he resumes his daily operator activities.

Adds Wolters:

> There is definitely a change in the culture and how it feels to come to work and what work means. The amount of loyalty, I would say, has been changed very much. I never had an intention of leaving before because wages were pretty competitive and the plant never had layoffs. Now, the competitive wages and financial security for my family are still there, but the base of my loyalty has shifted to where there is a certain level of feeling connected to the place where I work, and a certain level of ownership. That is very empowering.

Wolters says that not every day is perfect—he still feels moments of frustration—but his experience is a result of the engaging environment that CEO Dave Cote has tried to encourage.

6

Reward Them

Optimize Appreciation, Benefits, and Compensation

When employees feel well treated and taken care of,
they try to add value and grow the business.
—*Gamal Aziz, President and COO, MGM Grand*

n 2000, Egyptian-born hotelier Gamal Aziz left Las Vegas's Bellagio to become the executive vice president of hotel operations for MGM Grand, the hotel and casino whose gleaming emerald facade towers above The Strip. In less than a year, he was promoted to president and COO. MGM Grand was doing fine financially. Its family-friendly image and movie-themed attractions brought in $175 million in profit on revenues of $750 million. No one in management was complaining. As for workers, the majority were content. They came to work, did their jobs, and went home satisfied.

As president, Aziz's charge was to take the hotel to another level. His toughest hurdle, however, was a lack of one. Explains Aziz, "We were doing well enough that people thought, 'Why do we need to change?' My executive team had to overcome the we're-successful-so-why-are-you-messing-with-us attitude."

But Aziz knew external threats loomed. The MGM Grand brand risked becoming dated next to newer, trendier hotel-casinos like the Hard Rock Cafe and Mandalay Bay. And by 2010, Las Vegas could be short an estimated 25,000 workers. To overcome the competition and the inevitable talent crunch, MGM Grand had to do more than maintain its own status quo.

Aziz embarked MGM Grand on a more than $400 million revamp that entailed swapping the property's old-school brand for a more sophisticated, high-class blend of exclusive entertainment, distinctive dining, and hip suites. His goal was to create an impeccable visitor experience that Aziz dubbed Maximum Vegas. By any measure, Aziz has succeeded. By 2008, MGM Grand had become the world's largest hotel-casino, with 6,772 rooms and 36 restaurants, nightclubs, and stores, plus 4 enormous entertainment venues.

The crux of Aziz's plan hinged on an intangible element: transforming thousands of content employees into an energized, engaged workforce. If every employee went the extra mile in every single guest interaction—and when no one was watching—the results could be tremendous. "The hospitality business is called that for a reason," says Aziz. "When we survey guests, the very first thing they talk about is *how they are treated.*" Even at a place as flush with amenities as the MGM Grand, Aziz says that customers' first comments are not about their rooms' floor-to-ceiling views, the delicious lobster bisque from Craftsteak, or the dazzling Cirque du Soleil show. Guests talk about service, and that service is in the hands of every employee.

Says Aziz, "When an employee does not feel respected, well treated, and taken care of, the behavior displayed is carelessness, or just getting through the day, or avoiding getting into trouble . . . they do not seriously try to add value or create a culture that creates growth for the business. But when employees feel good about a company, they give it their all."

Employees who give it their all include food servers who do not just recite dinner specials, but recount how the king salmon arrived fresh from Seattle that morning. They include a concierge who doesn't just secure show tickets for guests, but ensures a seamless evening by rescheduling ticket holders' dinner reservations so they get to the theater on time. Going the extra mile means a guest services operator does whatever she can to find a violinist for a customer who wants to propose to his girlfriend in their suite. It means a blackjack dealer knows who's headlining at the amphitheater and if tickets are still available so he can inform his table players instead of saying, "I don't know," if they ask. Chefs that are engaged invent provocative menu items even during their off-hours, and butlers who give it their all patiently help hotel guests navigate their high-tech in-room entertainment systems—for the third time if requested. An engaged accounting administrator voluntarily attends management meetings so he can improve his understanding of the company's operations, and engaged executives routinely thank their administrative assistants at the end of each day.

To help MGM Grand's table dealers, chefs, housekeepers, concierges, servers, accountants, marketers, secretaries, and thousands of other employees feel good about the company, Aziz knows he has to prove that MGM Grand feels good about all of them. This does not require paying salaries that exceed gaming and hospitality industry norms. Aziz firmly believes that MGM Grand's pay needs to be at the going market rate, but he sees no need to go beyond that. Rather, MGM Grand focuses its resources on making employees feel special, cared for, even glamorous. Its reward program includes elements that really matter to MGM Grand's employees, including on-site, twenty-four-hour child care; on-site dental services; free, healthy meals at the cafeteria; weight-loss programs that pay for pounds lost; continued pay during military leave; red-carpet awards ceremonies; and health fairs that offer free medical consultations and screenings. MGM Grand was also among the first Vegas hotels or casinos to offer a 401(k) savings plan to all nonmanagement employees.

Its investment in employee rewards pays off in performance. Aziz succeeded in creating a first-class service establishment. His hotel and casino boasts more AAA Diamonds (fifty-four) than any hotel in America and houses more AAA Four Diamond restaurants under one roof than anyone in the United States. Between 2003 and 2007, Aziz oversaw eighteen consecutive quarters of revenue growth, thanks in part to double-digit increases in daily revenue per customer, revenue per room, and occupancy rates of 96 percent. The state's Hotel and Lodging Association also named Aziz Nevada's Hotelier of the Year in 2005.

These successes—all achieved since Aziz took the helm— emanate from employee attitudes like that of VIP services specialist Marlie Tabor: "There is only one philosophy for each guest: we must offer the best service that we can . . . people all come here for a reason, they want to enjoy their stay and they want to experience Maximum Vegas, which means going above and beyond." This type of attitude did not emerge in patches or of its own volition. This attitude was the outcome of Aziz's concerted effort to create it—and harness its power into strong performance.

Not coincidentally, MGM Grand's employee retention and engagement measurements are high. In 2006, average annual turnover was 16 percent among full-time employees, compared to an estimated 30 percent turnover rate at other Vegas properties, and 49 percent for the hospitality industry. And in 2005, when gaming icon Steve Wynn opened his new casino resort, only ninety-eight of MGM Grand's workforce—less than 1 percent—quit to work for him. Internal surveys reveal other telling signs of engagement:

- 92 percent of MGM Grand's almost 10,000 employees said they would recommend MGM Grand as a great place to work.
- 89 percent said their work had special meaning and was not "just a job."
- 89 percent said they planned to work at the organization until they retired.
- 90 percent of employees said they had feelings of respect and dignity; a sense of equity and fairness; and satisfaction with both their jobs and the work environment.

These successes result from efforts to Know, Grow, Inspire, and Involve workers, all of which are part of the deal to create an engaging work experience. But there's a final, crucial element of the deal as well—Rewards.

Optimize the ABCs of Rewards

Over the years, the working definition of Rewards has grown to include a long list of things that employers can offer workers in return for past performance and to encourage future effort. No longer just base salary, employers now generally view rewards as consisting of other forms of monetary recognition, such as annual bonuses, long-term incentives, stock and stock options. Rewards also include a basket of benefits, from health care and retirement savings plans to a range of things to help an increasingly time-constrained workforce manage time at work with the rest of their lives.

In the late 1990s, the notion of Rewards expanded further to include the nature of the work environment itself, in part because a wealth of research showed that the environment influences how employees feel about their jobs and the company they work for. We're not just referring to casual-dress days, free breakfast, and in-office game rooms popularized during the dot-com boom. We're talking about a bevy of elements that, together with pay and benefits, can make a significant and meaningful difference in an employee's total work experience, including formal awards and recognition programs, work-life balance policies, and mentoring programs.

Indeed, some companies use Total Rewards to refer to the entire work experience—both the financial *and* nonfinancial elements, including the types of things we just noted above and all of the things we highlighted about growing and involving employees. Other companies talk expansively about their "deal" with employees, to reflect the totality of what's offered to, and given by, both parties. Whatever the terms used, our Engaging Eight are exemplars of the philosophy that says the work experience is defined by the combination of four things on the Rewards front:

- Pay: what people are paid—and how fair and competitive their pay is.
- Benefits: how and to what extent people are protected from medical, financial, and other risks in their lives.
- Development: how the company will ensure their development and advancement.
- Environment: how supportive, stimulating, and open the culture and environment are day to day.

The challenge for most companies is to blend these elements together in a way that optimizes the value for both the company and employees. And by definition, the optimal blend of the Rewards package—or deal—is one that elicits the most positive reception from employees at the lowest cost for the employer. In other words, employees value what they're getting in proportion to the investment the company has made. Too often, this equation doesn't come together; the company finds itself investing too much in some areas that employees don't appreciate or need, while underinvesting in areas critically important to the workforce. And it's not always obvious what the high-appreciation elements will be.

Building the optimal Rewards program requires two steps. First, know the workforce, and understand what's valued most by different employee segments and how they would choose among all types of rewards. Second, evaluate value for cost. As noted, a program that generates significant value at a low cost for a lot of employees should be a prominent attribute of the total program. A very costly element that has moderate value may not play a significant role in the overall program.

We refer to this approach as "Total Rewards Optimization" because it allows a company to identify through statistical analysis which rewards will have the biggest impact on employee behavior and then create a package that delivers the highest return on the investment the company is making.

The approach relies on two tools. One is a market research-based survey method that asks employees to make trade-offs among various rewards. (The same method is used by automakers, for instance, to understand what attributes of a new car actually drive buyers' preferences.) This helps determine what's really most important to each individual and how their preferences affect their choice of rewards. We can see, for example, if employees would trade a small increase in base pay for a substantially higher bonus opportunity, or trade additional life insurance for the opportunity to get financial-planning advice. Through the choices employees make, companies learn which reward elements matter most and the impact those rewards are likely to have on various behaviors, like retention or engagement.

The second tool is a portfolio optimization assessment, which assesses the relative costs and savings associated with various combinations of rewards. When a company combines employee preference data with financial data, it can see the financial and behavioral impact of various reward packages and choose the ones that deliver the most perceived value to employees for the lowest cost.

In this chapter, we'll focus specifically on pay and benefits—along with what we believe is one of the most critical elements of the environment: appreciation. Think of this section as a quick tour of the ABCs of Rewards—Appreciation, Benefits, and Compensation.

The ABCs affect employee attitudes and behavior, albeit in different ways. For instance, appreciation probably has the most potential to increase engagement since it speaks directly to employees' emotional connection to the company. And while benefits and compensation don't usually engage employees in and of themselves, they support a number of other things that do—like career development practices. On the other hand, if they are poorly designed, communicated, or delivered, they can have a detrimental impact on employees. And if employees don't at least perceive their companies' pay and benefits to be in the range of competitive industry and regional standards, there's a good chance workers will *disengage*.

Together, the ABCs of Rewards can have a huge impact on people's engagement because they signal the company's level of interest in and focus on the workforce. In that sense, the ABCs directly support the number one engagement driver for workers in the United States and globally: the belief that senior management is sincerely interested in their well-being.

When it comes to the ABCs of Rewards, engaging companies do the following:

Show **KNOWLEDGEABLE APPRECIATION** that is small and spontaneous, as well as extravagant and expected.

OPTIMIZE BENEFITS to deliver health and financial security without breaking the bank.

Provide **COMPETITIVE COMPENSATION** programs that are fair and clearly communicated.

Acts of Appreciation

Engage people by acknowledging when they put forth significant extra effort or provide significant unexpected value. Appreciation, or recognition, is an incredibly powerful tool to touch people emotionally, and the ways to show appreciation range from small, spontaneous, inexpensive gestures to extravagant, generous awards. Engaging Eight organizations and their leaders have mastered both, as well as the gray area in between.

Some people worry that recognition efforts will be diminished if dispensed too often. But in our combined fifty years of experience in the workforce, we've never heard anyone say anything like, "There's just too much recognition around here. It doesn't mean anything." People across the organization—from customer service reps to technology support staff—can be influenced by recognition, and the following pages are flush with examples that may translate into your own work environment.

INFORMAL ACTS OF APPRECIATION

Informal acts of appreciation are in the hands of the recognizers—
the boss, the colleague, even the customer. Individual recognition
doesn't require approval from superiors, but it can be more formal
than just saying thanks. To be effective, such recognition should be
expressed soon after the event or activity that's being recognized occurs. Informal acts should not be scrimped and saved. Following is
a list of informal acts that you can incorporate into your management style if you're not yet doing so.

The Informed, Sincere Thank-You. At MGM Grand, President Gamal
Aziz tells his managers to be "knowledgeable admirers" of their
people. It's a simple concept with tremendous return. When you
compliment people on work well done, tell them *why;* use specifics
that let workers know you pay attention. Fact-based feedback engages people emotionally as well as rationally. Says Aziz, "I take every opportunity to articulate what people have done right. You get
more loyalty and devotion if you notice what is working versus what
is not working."

Aziz's staff agrees. Bette Gaines-Snyder is the director of MGM
Grand's slot and employee events: "I like to be appreciated and feel
that what I do every day is contributing to the success of the company."
Gaines-Snyder praises her direct reports the way Aziz praises her. "I
need to be specific about what they did," she says. After an event,
Gaines-Snyder sends group e-mails that articulate people's specific
contributions. "When I get the e-mails from Bette," says her colleague
Corrine Clement, "I feel that she was paying attention."

When workers see that their managers really get what they're
doing to help the company and colleagues succeed and take the time
to acknowledge it, employee engagement can soar.

This approach can also help build teams of high performers. In searching for the brightest leadership and management talent available, Aziz spans the globe and doesn't confine his search to other gaming or hospitality companies in Las Vegas or elsewhere in the United States. In Aziz's words, he wants to consistently find "people who are smarter than I am." He makes it his business to understand what they've done to succeed and what really drives them. In short, Aziz recruits people he admires. "I hire for intelligence over experience," he told us. Potential recruits feel his knowledgeable admiration and are quick to join.

The Personal Touch. Walk the floors of Campbell headquarters in Camden, New Jersey, and you'll see handwritten notes from CEO Doug Conant pinned to people's bulletin boards. Conant writes— with pen, not keyboard—some one hundred notes a week to employees at all levels. "If I were just sending e-mails, it would feel gratuitous and automatic. And in every note I try to recognize a specific thing," says Conant. The habit is contagious. Nancy Reardon, senior vice president and chief human resources and communications officer, sends handwritten notes to new employees before they start their jobs. The company even designs and prints its own thank-you cards—appropriately branded with product images such as Pepperidge Farm Goldfish on the front flap—for managers to use for their own staffs. Don't underestimate the power of personalized notes for even the most senior executives. Says Conant, "I worked at three wonderful companies for twenty-five years before I came to Campbell and received maybe three or four notes from the CEOs. I still have them. They're treasures to me."

There are many ways to personalize a thank-you. Just get to know a little bit about the people who work for you. REI's recognition gifts often reflect its employees' hobbies, such as mountain climbing or biking. At North Shore–LIJ, Emily Kao may bring her staff pizza to thank them for hard work. North Shore–LIJ also involves its employees' significant others in appreciation activities, by treating couples to a night out to celebrate significant milestones. EMC has followed a similar approach. In the first few months after EMC acquired the company Stephen Todd worked for, EMC treated Todd, his colleagues, and their significant others to a showing of *Phantom of the Opera* on Broadway in New York City. "Not in all my years at my former employer did someone thank me by treating me to a night out," recalls Todd, years later. "EMC knows how to reward us beyond anything my previous company knew how to do."

Face Time with the Boss. A lunch. A candid conversation. A handshake in front of peers. When bosses focus their valuable time and attention on one or a few individuals, it's a reward in itself. Campbell's Conant hosts a lunch in his office for workers several times a year. North Shore–LIJ CEO Michael Dowling routinely takes groups of workers to dinner and to hockey and baseball games. And whenever Dowling receives a letter of praise about an employee, he often goes to meet the worker in person, unannounced, and gives them a token, such as a gift certificate. "It's not the amount of the gift, but the fact that I personally told them I received a letter." Nance Dicciani, former president and CEO of Honeywell's Specialty Materials division, would walk into people's offices to say thanks and fly around the world to personally congratulate top performers at awards ceremonies.

The value of face time is universal. In India, the head of Honeywell's Technology Solutions Lab, Krishna Mikkilineni, observes, "Just spending time with employees and understanding what they are doing is important and makes people feel you are acknowledging their contributions. They feel good just because you took the time to listen and understand what they're working on. If someone does something extraordinary, just telling them it's appreciated matters more than any other kind of formal recognition."

At MGM Grand, Corrine Clement heads corporate communication and works directly with Aziz. "Some executives never page employees for good reasons, only for problems," says Clement. "The first time I got a page from Gamal, he was just calling to congratulate me on something. It was a compliment to get paged for something that was going right, and it set the tone for my future working relationship with Gamal." Clement responds to such gestures by being engaged and indispensable to the organization, often working into the night to prepare for the next day.

Public Praise. Give people credit in front of colleagues and superiors. When members of his executive team do an exceptional job, Novartis CEO Daniel Vasella tells his board of directors. Campbell's group director of public affairs, Judy Freedman, schedules recognition announcements before meetings begin so they don't get forgotten in the postmeeting wrap-up. When an MGM Grand housekeeper receives a complimentary letter from a guest, it's shared with her colleagues. MGM Grand also shows appreciation for workers in discrete departments by telling the rest of the workforce how that department contributes to the company's daily operations. At EMC, Kyle Leciejewski, a high-performing Millennial, has this to say about public praise:

> When you're out there busting your back and trying to do what's right for the customers, the company, and yourself, getting recognition for doing the right thing is very important. When I'm cited as a top sales representative on quarterly conference calls, when 50 people are on the line, or when I'm

called up in front of 200 people, that's as fulfilling and rewarding as other pieces . . .

Public praise with a purpose has a dual benefit. Beyond
encouraging the recognized employee to stay engaged, it encourages
colleagues to follow suit. Publicly recognizing how someone handled
a customer complaint or how someone worked with another
department sends an informed message to other colleagues that
those behaviors are important. Public praise reinforces leaders'
values, the organization's mission and vision, and the things that
count at the company.

Daily Thoughtfulness. Honeywell administrative assistant Marcia
Kiser feels recognized thanks to "lots of different ways my bosses let
me know that I'm appreciated. They let me go home early one day,
or on another day my boss will bring me back a KitKat bar, or they
might bring me breakfast. It's the small things that bring the team
together, and you know you are all pulling together for the big goal
of making money for the company and making customers happy."
These little acts can show people that someone cares about their
well-being, which, as we know, is the most important driver of employee engagement. Little acts can reflect your workers' preferences
and hobbies, such as tickets to their favorite baseball team or an afternoon off to see a son's soccer game.

Peer Recognition. Informal acts of appreciation are not only valued
when they come from above. Praise from colleagues—those both
next to us and below us on the proverbial ladder—can be very engaging. Nowhere did we hear about the power of peers more than at
EMC, where colleagues' expectations are high, and their feedback
carries a lot of meaning. "What motivates me is gaining respect

from my peers, as well as management," says Brad Morin, a thirty-six-year-old senior program manager. "That's part of our culture. We recognize when one of our teammates does a great job." If you want praise from peers, give it to others when deserved.

Make It Work. Simple acts of appreciation aren't second nature to every boss. But there are things companies can do to help managers make sure opportunities for small acts of appreciation don't slip away. For example, REI created what it calls a Recognition Tool Kit that makes it a breeze for even the most harried managers to regularly reward good work. The company distributes 360 gray plastic toolboxes decorated with stickers that read "You've Gone Above and Beyond." Inside the box reside themed gifts that can be handed out at the spur of the moment, like in-store coupons or chocolate carabiners (those oblong rings used for rock climbing). For managers with writer's block, REI has even preprinted words of gratitude on the inside of the thank-you notes and a pamphlet with guidelines about how to write a thank-you.

Individual acts of appreciation have perhaps the greatest ROI of any single action an organization does to reward employees. Says McKesson manager Todd Baldanzi, "It doesn't cost anything to give people credit." But the enhanced engagement that results is invaluable.

FORMAL ACTS OF APPRECIATION

Formal acts of appreciation are planned and programmatic. They range from department-level recognition to major organizational awards. And while they might not have the same personal feel as the day-to-day informal acts, they have a big effect on people. Even Michael Scott, the bumbling office manager at the fictitious Dunder

Mifflin depicted on NBC's sitcom *The Office* (a U.S. remake of the popular British comedy), understands this. In one episode, he explains that the day they award "The Dundee" is "everybody's favorite day." Says Scott, "Everybody looks forward to it because, you know, a lot of the people here don't get trophies very often . . ." Of course, formal acts of appreciation are not about the trophy. They are about the message. Here's a range of formal acts of recognition that we see:

Job- and Department-Specific Awards. These rewards come at regular intervals and focus on employee subgroups, such as sales. When an employee survey revealed that Campbell's administrative assistants did not feel valued, Deb Fair, the senior executive assistant for Campbell's president of global sales and chief customer officer, and some colleagues formed Campbell Administrative Professionals. The group created its own Ambassador of Excellence awards, and anyone in the company was allowed to nominate an administrator. In 2006, four winners out of seventy-two nominations were chosen. Each received $2,000, a plaque, an engraved Tiffany & Co. bracelet, and a personal letter from the CEO. Says Fair, "I believe it motivated those who were not nominated to continue to strive for excellence."

Customer-Driven Recognition. Satisfied customers are a prosperous source of engaging feedback, but don't assume they'll go out of their way to thank employees for stellar service. Formal programs can encourage customers to do so. For example, MGM Grand hosts hundreds of conventions each year, and upon arrival meeting planners receive between two and ten Gold Keys to pass out to MGM Grand workers who deliver exceptional service. The customer presents each Gold Key in a velvet bag to the employee, and employees return the key to the hotel's convention services department in exchange for an invitation to a quarterly Gold Key luncheon with MGM Grand's senior management.

American Airlines has a similar program for frequent fliers. As regular travelers ourselves, we've received packets of AAdvantage Recognition tickets that we could give to any employee we encountered at American who we thought delivered extraordinary customer service. If we didn't have that packet of recognition tickets, we may not have gone out of our way to acknowledge, say, the flight attendant who compassionately helped an elderly passenger get situated on the flight, talked with her about her concerns, listened to her attentively about her new grandchild, and helped her safely off the flight. It was exactly the way we would want a flight attendant to treat our parents, and we let the attendant know it. When the flight attendant read the comments on one of Julie's recognition tickets, she got tears in her eyes. "This is what makes me love my job," she said.

Peer-Driven Recognition. We noted above that praise from the people we work with—versus the people we work for—carries a unique emotional weight. Like an organization's customers, our colleagues are a rich source of recognition, which is why senior management should encourage peer recognition by formalizing it. EMC's R&R program invites employees to e-mail a few paragraphs about a colleague's performance worthy of public recognition. Submissions are reviewed and, at quarterly employee meetings, specific people are called out. At MGM Grand, employees nominate each other for Star of the Month awards, which recognize excellence in service and hospitality. Winners get a variety of Vegas-related perks, from cash and limo pickup and drop-off between home and work, to shopping sprees, extra vacations, even having their name in lights on MGM Grand's marquee.

Honeywell's Bravo awards allow line workers to recognize their peers. Each year, some 60,000 Bravos—brief descriptions of individual or team accomplishments—are e-mailed to colleagues and coworkers. And each week Honeywell picks an Everyday Hero from one of its global offices and plants. In Texas, administrative assistant Marcia Kiser's boss nominated her for an Everyday Hero award after Kiser helped collect on overdue invoices. Kiser was grateful after a company-wide e-mail praised her work: "I was stunned, surprised, and pleased when the e-mail came out because it was posted on Honeywell's internal website, and I heard from people I had not spoken to in years. It made me feel proud and very special. And, I was very surprised when I got an e-mail from our CEO. I was amazed, and shaking when I got the email. I thought, 'Wow, he pays attention . . .'"

ORGANIZATIONAL ACTS OF APPRECIATION

The Oscars of recognition awards, organizational acts of appreciation, are huge, both in the rewards themselves and in the meaning they carry. To be really effective, these awards must be granted with a level of rigor (winners should be evaluated by committees, not individuals); tied to business strategies (there should be evidence that winners furthered the organization's goals and embodied its values); and have participation and support from the most senior executives (the CEO can help select winners and present the award). Here are some examples:

- Each year, Campbell Soup Company awards $10,000 to a team or an individual to receive its Dr. John T. Dorrance Award, named after the company's founder. Some 200 employees are nominated each year for significantly contributing to business growth or success of a specific initiative, from community work to software implementation. In October 2007, forty awards were presented at Campbell's Extraordinary Performance Awards formal ceremony at Camden's Tweeter Center, a venue usually reserved for concerts. Campbell has turned the award process and ceremony into another opportunity for recognition; employees know it's an honor to be selected for the award's review committee or to be asked to cohost the ceremony. It's an emotional event. "People are amazingly touched by the honor and the recognition they receive," says chief human resources and communications officer Nancy Reardon. "Three years ago, an employee from a Belgium plant attended the ceremony. He had never traveled before. After the ceremony, he spoke to a small group of employees about what the day meant to him. Holding back tears, he told us that it was the most important day of his life."

Campbell's annual Influence of Honor Awards go to 350 people for exceptional leadership. Unlike the Dorrance award, these are not tied to individual business initiatives but behaviors. The ceremony is held at prestigious venues, such as Boston's John F. Kennedy Presidential Library or the Philadelphia Museum of Art. Says Campbell's senior vice president of public affairs, Jerry Buckley, "You want awards to be bulletproof. People look at who has been given awards so you want to make sure they are truly deserving because they will be watched and admired."

- REI's annual Anderson Awards, named after the co-op's founder, go to an employee at each of the retailer's locations—about one hundred winners per year who each demonstrate the company's core values. Winners get a paid three-day trip to REI's headquarters in Washington State, where they meet with senior executives, go hiking, preview new products, and receive a plaque from the CEO at an emotion-packed dinner. "There is not a dry eye in the house," one employee told us. "And when the winners go back to their workplaces, they share their experiences with coworkers."

- Each year at North Shore–LIJ, three major awards are given. The Exceptional Patient Experience Award goes to a single employee who went "above and beyond the expectations of his or her assigned role." The Innovation Award goes to the person or team that demonstrated entrepreneurial spirit by creating a new process or program with measurable improvements to patient service or the quality of clinical care. Finally, the Team Award goes to a collaborative work group that improved the patient experience, operations, and/or financial performance. Note that each award is directly linked to the health system's strategic initiatives of customer service, process innovation, and collaboration.

- Each month, MGM Grand selects one Star of the Month winner from twelve nominees from each of its major divisions. Monthly winners get $700, their name in lights on MGM Grand's marquee on The Strip, a VIP parking spot for a month, and their photo on a wall of fame outside the employee dining room. Marlie Tabor, the VIP services specialist who started her MGM Grand career as a keno writer, explains how being named employee of the month increased her own engagement. "When I go to work I just think I have to do more because people look at me as to how [well] I do my job . . . I have a reputation to live up to, and the award makes me work harder."

At the end of each year, MGM Grand honors the twelve winners with an extravagant black-tie gala, where one of the twelve is named Star of the Year. Before and during the gala, honorees are treated like celebrities: A limo takes them to a local mall where they shop for tuxedoes or gowns and accessories to wear to the event, all paid for by MGM Grand. Each honoree and a guest arrive at the gala in a limousine, walk down a red carpet, pose for paparazzi, and are interviewed by MGM Grand's own TV crew. Dinner for 1,800 includes a private concert by a well-known entertainer, videos that showcase each Star of the Month, and more prizes (a trip for two, a week off with pay, a $1,500 check). The employee named Star of the Year receives an additional $1,500.

MGM Grand's appreciation initiatives succeed because they not only reflect truly good work, but treat workers with the fun and glamour they spend their days providing others. In this vein, appreciative acts should reflect the culture and values of the working population, be they demographic or psychographic.

At Novartis's offices in Korea, for example, the company's former country head Andrin Oswald (who is currently head of global development franchises) knew it was important for Korean workers to have their successes frequently celebrated and quantified in front of colleagues. "Giving money to show recognition has a strong historic tradition," he says. As country head of Korea, Oswald doled out some twenty-five awards during each quarterly meeting, linking each to a financial contribution that translated into financial compensation. A designated Team Spirit budget paid for employees to go out and celebrate.

What about all the employees who aren't formally recognized? Does lack of public praise have the potential to disengage them? While there's a small risk of alienating someone who feels he deserved the award instead of someone else, the scale tips in favor of rewarding top performance and recognizing people who can serve as role models. Inevitably, some people will feel unappreciated, but the majority will strive to mirror the excellence that the organization values. To minimize feelings of exclusion, ensure that the workforce is well informed about the company's various reward programs, from small to large, and is well versed in what it takes to be nominated and to win. And, make sure winners deserve it.

Appreciation is truly in a company's power to control and differentiate. "There has always been a need to catch people in the act of doing something right," says REI employee programs coordinator Carolyn Iwata. "The way you do it does not have to be elaborate, as long as it is personal."

Optimize Benefits for Health and Financial Security, and Gain Advantage with a Focus on Work-Life Balance

While senior executives and front-line managers don't have to absorb the technical complexities of benefits program operations, understanding the basics is important. Leaders at all levels play a very significant role in how people perceive and value their benefits—and, by implication, their belief that the company cares about them. Leaders should view benefits from the company's perspective as well as through employees' eyes so they can help people understand what they're getting, how their benefits work, and how those benefits fit in the total mix of investments the company is making in them.

Companies have always had to consider benefits through two sometimes competing lenses: cost management and workforce management. Specifically, organizations have to provide competitive benefits to recruit and retain workers at a cost that enables them to maintain profitability and compete effectively on the global stage. It sounds pretty straightforward, but according to research Towers Perrin published in 2007, few organizations think they're walking this tightrope very well. Most of the executives surveyed didn't think their benefits programs were effectively achieving cost-management objectives or supporting the kind of organizational culture needed to drive strong business results. Ironically, though, they did think their companies were doing a good job meeting employee needs.

Employees themselves adamantly disagreed with the executives. They found benefits lacking and did not fully appreciate the value provided by their health care and other benefits. These differing perspectives suggest companies are investing a lot and getting minimal—or no—return.

The study showed something else, though. Employees want and need help in managing their own health care and in planning for retirement, and they understand that help doesn't have to be in the form of financial support. If companies provide a different type of assistance—through initiatives such as education and tools to help employees make better decisions about their benefits, their health care, and their long-term retirement needs—then they can improve the return on their investment and get benefits "right."

Benefits programs that are confusing, perceived as unfair, inaccessible, or poorly administered can undermine people's relationships with their employer. Just think of some of the people portrayed in Michael Moore's movie *Sicko,* about the nature of America's health care system. The film featured one woman transported to an emergency room in an ambulance after a car accident. Unfortunately, her insurance company declined her medical claim because she didn't get the ambulance ride preapproved. Other people in the film related tales of tumors that were not covered by insurance because their health plans denied treatment for preexisting conditions, experimental treatments, or lack of medical

necessity. While many of the examples in the movie are extreme
cases Moore used to illustrate shortfalls of the U.S. health insurance
industry, they also act as a warning flag for employers: employees
might direct their own frustrations with the nation's health care
system toward the organization for which they work. One way to
avoid such negative transference is to ensure that benefits programs
are as well designed and as easy to use as possible.

Well-designed benefits programs support another engagement
driver: an organization's reputation for social responsibility. Being a
good corporate citizen is about showing respect and contributing to
the world outside the organization's walls, but corporate citizenry is
hollow unless it includes its own workforce. When an organization
covers the basic needs for employee security and provides support
for employees to realize their personal and financial potential—as
the Engaging Eight do in a variety of fashions—its reputation both
locally and afar can be an engaging source of pride.

To get benefits right, organizations should look at them from
four perspectives by asking the following questions:

- *Access:* What kind of benefits should the organization offer?
- *Cost sharing:* What level of protection should the organization
  provide, and how much of the cost should it pay?
- *Ease of use:* Is the program easy to understand and use? Are
  tools and materials available to support it?
- *Work-life support:* Does the benefits program help people stay
  healthy and balanced today and prepare for their financial
  future?

Engaging organizations distinguish themselves from others by
the degree to which they address each of these four perspectives—or

how they answer the questions. Most employers focus primarily on access and cost sharing because they have an obvious impact on the bottom line. Far fewer employers look at ease of use and work-life support, which are the very things that can prevent employee dissatisfaction or confusion, and increase the value workers assign to the company's overall benefits program.

Engaging organizations treat each of the four attributes as equally important. And, as you'll see, getting the four attributes correct is a distinguishing feature in the quest for employee engagement.

ACCESS

Access is about deciding which benefits to make available to which groups of employees. Having access to benefits is, in and of itself, valuable to many people. That's because companies have more clout and resources than individuals, and thus can provide benefits that may not be available to individuals in the retail market, or available to them at an affordable cost. By simply providing access, even without contributing any money, an organization can offer something employees need or want. And for every benefit an organization decides to make available, it sends an essential message to employees: we understand you must deal with things in your life, and we want to help.

An excellent example is Engaging Eight organization REI, which delights workers by meeting the needs of employee groups not traditionally covered by health and retirement benefits. For example, REI is one of the few retailers that offer part-time workers health care coverage—at a cost to the employee of about $15 per paycheck— as well as paid vacation and sick leave. Says Michelle Clements, REI's senior vice president of HR:

It was an amazing thing to watch when we rolled out health care insurance to part-timers. The real story was the impact it had on full-timers and management team members, who felt uncomfortable, like the haves and the have-nots. Half of our employees are part-time, and the full-time workers remember what it was like when they were part-time. So when we extend that benefit it makes the work environment feel more fair and supportive. It sends the message that we are not paternalistic, but that we care about employees and are going to do the right thing.

At REI's flagship store, general manager Rachel Ligtenberg is insured via REI's life-partner benefits. REI was one of the first companies in the United States to offer domestic partnership coverage to same-sex and opposite-sex partners. Says Ligtenberg, "HR approached me in the early 1990s and asked what life-partner benefits would mean to me. It makes me proud that REI was a pioneer in this area." Ligtenberg and her partner have also adopted two children and used REI's adoption benefits—up to $3,000 reimbursement to apply toward adoption costs. Says Ligtenberg, "This has me feeling as if I am also appreciated and rewarded as a whole person. In the same way, I want to extend those benefits to my team and engage them as whole people. I think benefits can further endear employees to the extent that this is a place where the best and the brightest will choose to invest their intellect and passion."

Benefits such as part-time or life-partner health care convey to all REI's employees—not just those whom health plans cover—that senior management cares about every one of its workers, which helps position REI as a good corporate and community citizen. In turn, the needs of discrete populations are being met.

COST SHARING

In today's cost-conscious environment, designing benefits programs to meet employee needs at an affordable cost for the employer is a major challenge—and one that's not going away. To get this balance right, companies need to consider a range of factors: the competitive market and what others in their industry or region are offering; employees' perspective on what they do or don't need or value; and employees' degree of comfort with the risk they need to shoulder for expenses in the event of illness, other health conditions, or, ultimately, retirement.

Offering employees choices among different types of benefits—a so-called flexible benefits approach—is one way to address their varied needs. And, establishing a clear and transparent philosophy on how costs are shared can send strong, positive messages.

EASE OF USE

Although benefits should be easy to understand and convenient to access and use, surprisingly, this often isn't the case. If benefits plans don't meet these core ease-of-use requirements, employees often grumble about their benefits and feel their company doesn't care enough. Several factors contribute to benefits' ease of use:

- Simple design.
- Clear communication of design and philosophy.
- Education and support tools.
- Efficient benefit processing and problem resolution.

Benefits programs with an expansive array of features and conditions can do more to confuse than support employees. Nearly two-thirds of respondents in our last *Global Workforce Study* rated their organizations "fair" or "poor" in providing clear benefits (and pay) information. And in focus groups, employees tell us time and time again that they don't find value in overly complex benefits programs. In many cases they don't even realize the specific benefits they're being offered. Worse, employees may feel they were cheated because a benefit limit seemed to be unclear, hidden, or not understood until the insurance company declined a submitted expense.

Communicating benefits is an ongoing struggle as employers try not to overwhelm and confuse employees while providing essential program information. To clearly communicate benefits, including their limitations, engaging organizations invest time to do so, often creating additional, easy-to-understand materials, illustrative examples, and ultimately making an informed person or people readily available to employees so their questions can be quickly and easily answered. Recall the preceding chapter, when we described how North Shore–LIJ's Carol Battaglia helped to reorganize the human resources department to be more responsive to the hospitals' employees—HR's internal customers—to reduce their frustration and any unintended fallout on patients. At MGM Grand, full-time, informed employees man a consumer-friendly benefits office; they stand behind a counter, ready and willing to help employees answer any benefit-related questions.

As more benefits responsibility and costs shift to employees, there's an even greater need for benefits education and support tools. This is particularly true when it comes to helping employees manage their health and financial security. For health care, the best way to avoid cost is to stay healthy, and organizations can help teach their people how to do so by providing tools and incentives that encourage people to make healthy choices. Health fairs, for example,

let employees learn about their own health risks and options. Cafeterias that offer a wide variety of low-fat, low-sodium choices make
it easier for people to eat well. Visible and leader-supported charity
walks, fun runs, and other physical activities are more likely to draw
employee participation. MGM Grand, as you'll recall, provides a
variety of support and reinforcement for keeping employees healthy,
including flu shots, cholesterol tests, on-site mammogram screenings, in-house dental services, weight-loss programs that pay for
each pound lost, smoking-cessation classes, and wearable gadgets
that record the number of steps a worker walks each day to encourage
people to walk more.

EMC has perhaps been the most innovative in its adoption of a
consumerism philosophy toward health care. The multibillion-dollar
technology organization is in the process of restructuring its entire
health care delivery system for its 35,000 employees. Gaining in
popularity, consumerism revolves around the notion that employees
should take more responsibility for managing both their health and
their health care, supported by tools and information the employer
can provide. And this means tools beyond health fairs.

Specifically, EMC gives all employees their own online health
records in which they can enter personal health information and
have it integrated with health claims information. The online
system, hosted by WebMD, also provides employees with information they can use to make health decisions. As Jack Mollen,
EMC's executive vice president in charge of HR—and HR Executive
of the Year in 2006—explains:

> To be an innovative company, you must innovate in all areas,
> not just products. We believe all leaders must innovate in their
> own space, so [HR] had to change the way it manages people's
> health care.

The imperative was clear. For years we saw health care costs grow by some 15 percent annually, and today our health care costs go up in the low single digits, about 6 percent to 7 percent, half the cost for competitors in our industry. We credit this to consumerism. Consumerism requires that people have access to and "own" their own health care information so they get ahead of their health care problems. It also requires that employees provide information by taking a "risk analysis" and signing up for the program so their individual doctors and health care providers can post their medical information in one place. That place is a confidential database hosted and run by WebMD, a company we partner with, which collects all our employees' health care information in one place and puts it in a format. Individual information is only accessible by the employee; EMC can only see aggregate data. We call it a personal health record, something each employee can access and understand. WebMD also provides our employees informed intelligence on health care options, like the trade-off between a brand name or generic prescription drug. They can log on and find out what kind of healthy lifestyle might be able to eliminate problems they have. We feel very strongly that if we give our employees information and encourage them to use it, they will.

As a result, our people are becoming smarter consumers of health care.

EMC is so committed to this approach that employees who did not sign up to have all their medical data consolidated into the online health record were told their own health care costs would rise 12 percent. EMC says only 2 percent of its workforce does not participate.

EMC is taking the same consumerism approach to employees' financial benefits, working with Fidelity to invent a wealth-creation website exclusively for EMC employees. Explains Mollen, "As an employer, EMC gives employees many different avenues to create wealth, but it's the responsibility of the employee to utilize those tools so he or she can retire at the same standard of living that he or she enjoyed while working." Ideally, all EMC employees would have a personal wealth record that consolidates all of their financial vehicles, from company 401(k)s and stock options to bank accounts and other investments not related to EMC. Like the personal health record, this financial information would be private (EMC could never access individual information, only consolidated data for the workforce as a whole) and portable, so employees could take the information with them if they left the company.

Helping employees manage financial benefits is both a short- and long-term proposition. Many employees have little to no idea how much money they'll need in retirement, and even less of an idea of how to use the employer plans to save. Engaging employers such as EMC offer tools to help estimate future financial needs and provide experts to help people understand various savings and investment options.

WORK-LIFE SUPPORT

This fourth attribute truly separates the best in class. Benefits that make employees' lives more manageable support productivity and enhance people's daily perception of how the organization feels about them.

In thinking about work-life support, companies need to consider two distinct areas: (1) their vision for themselves as corporate citizens and their role regarding social responsibility and (2) employee opinions about how their personal needs affect their productivity and ability to balance work and personal responsibilities. For example, employers who champion diversity should ensure that their own practices serve the needs of different demographic groups within their population. The needs may span age, education, ethnicity, family status, physical limitations, or geography.

Only when an employer takes time to Know its workforce can it fully understand people's concerns and select and package programs to meet those identified needs. In many cases, this is not a matter of investing more money, but investing a bit more time in thoughtful design and delivery.

At Novartis, employee opinion surveys revealed some discontent among working parents at its headquarters in Basel, Switzerland—mainly mothers—when it came to their ability to effectively balance job responsibilities with child care needs. To identify specific reasons for their discontent, Novartis's HR team e-mailed 800 employees with children and invited them to participate in focus groups. For those who couldn't attend, HR asked them to answer a few questions about their child care needs via e-mail. Some 70 employees attended two focus groups, and 600 responded to questions. The anecdotal and survey data revealed two overriding problems: too much child care expense and not enough flexibility.

First, Novartis's on-site, subsidized child care facilities did not have enough space for all the children who needed care, forcing parents to go elsewhere and spend more money. HR told the pharmaceutical division's executive committee, which responded immediately and approved construction of expanded child care facilities on the corporate campus, as well as additional child care subsidies. The entire process—from focus groups to executive approval of spending—took an impressive three months.

What's more, parents working at Novartis did not feel the organization's hard-charging culture—and their direct supervisors—always supported the day-to-day flexibility that working parents required. This was a more complex issue than simply increasing the number of child care slots, and by no means exclusive to Novartis. Many parents told Novartis's HR team that work-life balance could be difficult because, for example, bosses might schedule group meetings at or after 5 p.m., the hour child care typically ends. "Most global companies that are high performing struggle with this notion of work-life balance and flexibility," says Michelle Gadsden-Williams, vice president and global head of diversity and inclusion. "As a company we are working hard to embrace it."

Child care benefits are just one of the ways a company can give working parents the flexibility they need to make time for their families. Telecommuting options (from working at home one day a week to the freedom to leave the office from time to time without fear of backlash) are other potentially low-cost benefits that contribute to an employee's sense of work-life balance and overall well-being. And, they are also benefits that supervisors in particular have a direct opportunity to influence, especially when they understand that flexibility does not imply employees will work less, just that they will work differently—and often more efficiently.

Engaging organizations also provide a mix of self-help tools—seminars, books, health fairs, access to external resources, on-site dentists, mammogram vans—that not only make a benefits plan more effective, and more useful and practical, but offer employees an additional level of personal support and security. Show a worker how to lower his cholesterol and stop smoking, and he will feel more secure about his physical future. Help an employee calculate how much money she needs to save to buy a home, and that knowledge and the corresponding monthly budget will prove another source of stability. Offer free mammogram screenings fifty feet from a worker's office, and she'll be more likely to benefit from early detection of cancer, or feel secure after learning her results were negative. Not all employees will take advantage of self-help tools—they may never use the fitness center or attend retirement-planning sessions—but knowing that the tools are available conveys the sense that senior management cares enough to provide them.

Our latest research underscores how closely employees' views of their benefits are intertwined with the number one engagement driver: employees' belief that the organization cares about their well-being. When we analyze and compare survey results, we find that employees who believe the company cares about their well-being are also much more likely to feel that benefits programs meet their needs. So, while benefits don't necessarily drive engagement, how benefits and benefit changes are managed and communicated can positively influence—or seriously undermine—the kind of trust crucial to engaging the workforce.

Provide Competitive Compensation That Is Fair and Clearly Communicated

Money is not a major driver of employee engagement. Neither the size of a paycheck nor a raise or bonus motivates employees over the long term. They may well put a bounce in someone's step for a few weeks, but eventually that higher pay becomes a new baseline.

Pay is, however, a significant factor—indeed, the most significant factor—in attracting workers and an important element in retaining them. Respondents to our *Global Workforce Study* rated "competitive base pay" as the number one reason they join an organization; "fair compensation" was the sixth most important factor affecting their decision to stay. But pay was not even among the top ten drivers of engagement.

Once companies hit the right level of pay, they get to a point where base salary increases don't drive different behavior. Companies that do not understand this often intensify their own financial burden by boosting employee pay with the expectation that enhanced performance will follow. Then, they're surprised when it doesn't. That said, failing to hit the right compensation levels is hazardous to an organization's health. When employees perceive pay as uncompetitive or unfair, any uptick in engagement stemming from efforts to Grow, Involve, and Inspire begin to erode. So while pay may not affect how much an employee voluntarily gives above and beyond what is expected of him, poor pay—real or perceived—can reduce his level of overall effort.

When it comes to compensation, an overriding rule is to *avoid disengagement*. Organizations and managers need to get pay right because the alternative has damaging consequences—decreased loyalty, decreased dedication, decreased effort. To get it right, companies should adhere to three guidelines:

- Pay must be in a *competitive* range compared to the industry and local market.
- Pay must be perceived as *fair*, especially by high performers.
- Pay policies and related performance expectations must be *clearly communicated*.

CEOs agree. Not one of the leaders among the Engaging Eight organizations said their strategy was to outpay the competition. Here's what some of them said about their own pay philosophies:

- Doug Conant, Campbell Soup Company: "Our philosophy is to competitively compensate our executives and pay for performance. Most of the 'value' for our senior executives comes from long-term compensation, and that is directly linked to our total shareholder returns relative to our peer group. When I started working here, a lot of people's [stock] options were under water. Everyone I recruited here was already successfully moving forward with their careers. But they were also at a point where they wanted to do something special. Does that mean they would work for free? No. They wanted to be competitively compensated, but they were also willing to bet that they could help contribute to one of the most compelling turnarounds in the history of our industry. Remember, when we started this journey, our company was being called the next 'buggy whip' of the food industry. Clearly, if the executives were in it exclusively for the money, there were a lot of higher-paying, safer employment opportunities beyond the four walls of Campbell. Encouragingly, the turnaround is well under way, and the compensation is reflecting our progress."

- Joe Tucci, EMC: "I am a huge pay-for-performance fan. You want the best people, and if you want them to work extraordinarily hard, I think you have to put the motivation there. You will be paid very well at EMC if you are successful, and you will also have the opportunity to share in the value we create for shareholders."

- Michael Dowling, North Shore–LIJ Health System: "Money is important, but it is not the whole package. At the end of the day, people want to work in a place that gives them an opportunity to advance, a place where they do good work. We pay well, but there are constraints; you can do a lot of other things to make a difference, like showing people you appreciate them."

- Dave Cote, Honeywell International: "We have to be competitive from a salary and cost standpoint. Everyone always wants to say it is the softer things that matter, and it's true, they do matter, but if you are not paying someone appropriately, it is tough for someone to say they would rather take care of the company than take care of their family . . . if people see that everyone gets paid the same no matter how they perform, then they will all perform the same."

- Dr. Daniel Vasella, Novartis: "Most people are generally motivated to contribute, and the very important thing is to have clarity of objectives, fairness in evaluations, and fairness in compensation . . . if people think they are being treated fairly, it is very motivating . . . fairness does not mean softness in any way or shape, but it means people feel the process of evaluation is fair and the outcome is fair."

Not once did employees tell us that they felt engaged because they made a certain amount of money. Rather, they agree with their CEOs and reinforce the company's pay philosophies, as illustrated with these representative comments directly from employees:

- Nancy Reagan, VP of Wal-Mart team, Campbell Soup Company: "Pay is important, no doubt about it, but why I stay is because of the recognition. The financial piece gets me to the table, but it goes way beyond that. Frankly, I could probably get the same compensation from another company, but I like that I am empowered to do my job, that I am recognized for what I do."
- Stephen Todd, developer, EMC: "Honestly, money is less of an issue for me. It's more important that when I get up in the morning I want to enjoy what I do . . . I also really value work-life balance. As much as I say I enjoy my job and am proud

and happy to work here, going home and hitting ground balls
to my kid is better. And so I have been able to do that. I never
ever had a situation where anyone at EMC said, 'No, you can't
go to your son's Little League game or your daughter's recital.'
It's always been, 'Hey, go ahead. I'm sure you'll end up making
up the work another way.'"

As Stephen Todd's sentiments imply, pay is not as engaging as
the work itself and the flexibility he has to enjoy family. However,
Todd also told us that his overall compensation package is
competitive, which reduces the chances of his actively even looking
for another job.

Pay Competitively

Most organizations aspire to pay competitively. They want actual
employee pay to be positioned around the market rate, which is the
most common rate of pay for a given job.

Most large employers have standard processes for gathering and
analyzing market data. They generally have access to salary surveys
for the jobs in the markets where they recruit. HR departments can,
and do, check the market periodically to ensure that their pay is not
out of line externally, and they build internal salary structures to
both replicate that market and have a rationale to determine the pay
of their employees. Since most markets have grown 2 percent to 3
percent annually for the last decade, the prudent employer checks
the market about every three years. Companies in particularly hot
industries need to check regional pay levels more often, as well as
pay for jobs that are troublesome to fill. The best way to discern
whether the organization's pay is not competitive is via patterns of
higher-than-average attrition.

PAY FAIRLY

When people think about their compensation, they do not think about the exact amount of pay as much as consider whether their pay is *fair*. For most workers, "fair" has a comparative connotation that can be summed up by behavioral psychologist John Stacy Adams's Equity Theory, which proposes that people feel fairly compensated when the ratio of their contributions to rewards is the same as the ratio of others' contributions to rewards.

How does one determine the value of an employee's contribution? The definition of value is relative to each organization. As we discussed in Grow, some jobs are inherently more valuable than others because, for example, they directly contribute to overall revenue or earnings. Value can be measured two ways. One is quantitative—the knowledge and skills required to do a job as well as how much revenue someone brings in, for example—the WHAT. The other is qualitative—the type of behavior someone displays in their decisions and interactions on a regular basis—the HOW. If value is defined as a combination of WHAT is achieved and HOW it is achieved, and if employees are paid according to the level of value they deliver, pay will be deemed fair.

It is not easy to reward both WHAT and HOW with equal weight. In our experience, the biggest obstacle toward rewarding star performers with additional pay is the boss's discomfort with giving poorer performers less pay. Pay-for-performance requires some painful choices—especially for managers—such as firing high-revenue generators who fail to play by ethical rules, or withholding pay from pleasant, collegial workers whose contributions lag those of colleagues. Still, one of the most disengaging things any supervisor can do is to pay everyone in the same job the same amount of money. The poor performers may be thrilled, but high performers will check out emotionally, assuming they even stay on board. When inconsiderate behavior or underperformance is rewarded, high performers who play by the rules perceive the pay process as unfair and will become demotivated.

Distributing performance-based pay increases is not easy for many direct managers. Many simply feel uncomfortable giving some people less money than others, or holding back on the amount of a base-pay increase. It's tough to pinpoint why, but a lot of supervisors equate base-pay increases with cost-of-living increases and their workers' ability to pay the mortgage. They feel it's required to ensure that workers at least stay whole with the cost of living. That's understandable, but will lead to lack of differentiation and enormous dissatisfaction among high performers. As well, it is difficult to create meaningful differentiation with the modest pay increase budgets of most companies.

One way to resolve this dilemma is to provide performance-based pay in forms other than in base salary. Yes, top performers should still get a higher percentage increase in base pay, but there are other ways to reward people who bring the most value to the organization. These include promotions (which come with a higher pay increase, usually about 10 percent to 15 percent versus the single-digit rise in base pay without a promotion); special recognition accompanied by a monetary reward; or higher variable pay, such as bonuses or stock grants. Managers are much more comfortable holding back on variable pay for poor performers because, unlike base salary, it is viewed as an "extra" based on performance.

Do not limit pay-for-performance to individuals. All employees can be rewarded when their work group and the organization as a whole perform well. REI's three-pronged incentive-pay plan gives all workers—who are also members of REI's co-op structure—a bonus when individuals, departments, and/or the company reach performance goals. The actual dollar amount of each worker's bonus depends on that individual's pay, but all employees, even part-timers, are eligible. While base wages for store employees are set to be competitive with the local market, REI's group-oriented pay-for-performance strategy gives REI a competitive edge.

"Most retailers care only about individual performance, and it creates a competition for commissions," says Michelle Clements, REI's senior vice president of HR. "I argue that our recognition effort is about collaboration: everyone is focused on what is good for the store and ultimately the customer. People do not work on commission. We do not feel that would be a healthy element to team-based culture." Paying employees relative to the value of performance should be the core compensation strategy for every organization. To be done right, pay-for-performance requires having metrics in place that truly distinguish performance levels and articulate different pay scales.

Whatever your pay plan, don't break the rules. Employees expect their bosses to adhere to company-wide policies and to deliver compensation fairly.

CLEARLY COMMUNICATE PAY POLICIES AND RELATED PERFORMANCE EXPECTATIONS

People need to know that there is an organization-wide pay program in place. They want to know supervisors tie pay increases to organizational pay policies and individual performance. Communication is the best way to avoid disengagement caused by compensation. Unfortunately, not enough organizations actually communicate the components of their pay system to employees, which is why there tends to be a lot of mystery and intrigue—as well as misunderstanding—around pay.

In a 2006 employee survey, 41 percent of employees in McKesson Corp.'s Medical-Surgical division ranked their pay as "favorable," a percentage HR and senior management felt should be higher because total compensation was, indeed, competitive. "We did more in-depth studies and found nothing out of kilter. It was all about their perception, and we just needed to change their perception using factual data," says McKesson's organizational effectiveness consultant Randi Claytor. McKesson Medical-Surgical didn't give an across-the-board pay raise, but rather began to formally educate workers about the well-researched pay strategy so they understood how supervisors determined salaries each year. HR developed a compensation training presentation that spelled out McKesson's pay-for-performance philosophy and explained the industry and geographic research that went into determining salaries for various jobs and performance levels.

"We do not want compensation to be a black hole," says Claytor. "We want it to be transparent so every employee is knowledgeable and truly understands how they are being paid and how we reward individuals for the contributions they make." About half of McKesson Medical-Surgical's national workforce was exposed to a frank compensation presentation and explanation via seminars. Says Claytor, "We told them we heard loud and clear that a lot felt underpaid, and while we were not in a position to just give everyone pay increases, we wanted them to understand the process we go through to ensure we provide competitive wages, and we hoped it would make a difference."

It did. On McKesson Medical-Surgical's mid-2007 employee survey, favorable pay perceptions jumped ten points, to 51 percent, just months after education began. McKesson Medical-Surgical's educational initiative speaks to one of the top reasons that pay, when fair, may be perceived otherwise: employees may just not understand why it is what it is.

Explaining pay policies also falls to individual supervisors. Even if senior management and HR construct a well-designed pay program that they take pains to explain, supervisors are the ultimate harbingers of corporate policy. When direct bosses discuss employee performance in detail, frequently, and honestly, the overall compensation and rewards process is more likely to be perceived as fair. But when people get promoted or even receive salary increases and do not know why, it doesn't really feel like a victory. That's why delivering informed performance reviews is part and parcel of delivering fair pay. Indeed, pay and performance management depend to a great extent on the skills and abilities of *every single supervisor* to set goals, provide feedback, and determine pay levels.

Every organization needs to train supervisors not only to explain and administer pay, but to deliver engaging performance reviews. Engaging reviews do three things well. First, they clearly define what is expected of employees to be top performers—this includes identifying WHAT they must deliver as well as HOW they should deliver it. This harkens back to the Grow chapter, where we discussed the importance of linking employee education opportunities with specific behaviors, skills, and information that most contribute to success. The same can be said for pay. Compensation should be clearly linked to workplace actions and behaviors that drive value and growth and make a real difference to results, and employees should be very clear on what these are.

At Honeywell, all employees, including the CEO, are told by their direct manager that they will be rated on how well they exhibit each of the same twelve behaviors (which include focusing on customers, getting results, and fostering teamwork). Supervisors rate each behavior at one of three levels: Exceed, At, or Below. An employee's ranking determines the level of merit increase in base pay, as well as his or her bonus. "People who underperform or do not have the right behaviors can receive nothing," says Honeywell's Mary Anne Robinson, a vice president in human resources. "Those who exceed are eligible for the top end of the merit increase." Because each Honeywell employee knows what he will be judged against, he also understands the rationale behind his pay. That was not always the case. "My first couple of years here [before CEO Dave Cote], I would get a 5 percent raise and have no idea why," recalls Robinson. "Now it's very clear why we get what we get . . . you either did or did not achieve your results or exhibit the twelve behaviors."

Second, performance discussions should occur more than once a year, although not all meetings must be as thorough as an official year-end review. At Campbell, managers are asked to check in with employees quarterly. Mary Lemonis, Campbell's director of global organization effectiveness, says midyear and quarterly discussions maintain momentum and track progress so there are no surprises at the end of the year, when a formal review is linked to potential pay increases. Some Campbell managers even meet monthly with their direct reports.

Third, supervisors must be honest when discussing people's strengths and weaknesses related to the job's requirements and an employee's own career goals. Honest performance reviews trickle down from the top, and managers too often review their employees in a manner similar to how their boss reviewed them. "I am very candid on the really good things I see and the things I would like to see done differently," says Honeywell CEO Dave Cote on how he reviews his executive team. "If I cannot do it with my team, how can I expect them to do it with their folks, and so on and so on."

Perceived fairness in pay and performance reviews does not

solely depend on the absolute dollars employees get, but on how the pay and reviews are communicated to employees, by both the organization and the direct supervisor. People want to understand what is expected of them, how they met or failed to meet those expectations, and be paid accordingly.

As with all other engaging initiatives, compensation procedures must be supported from the top of the organization, not just dictated by HR. The CEO needs to make sure there is an up-to-date deal and employment philosophy that truly differentiates people by the value of their contributions and reflects market pay rates. CEOs should evaluate and promote their own direct reports based on performance. A CEO's decisions are scrutinized. If he rewards executives for tenure alone, for example, not only will newly hired high performers flee, but an "if I just hang on until I can retire" mentality may take root.

Finally, the CEO's own pay—a highly visible, widely scrutinized, and often misunderstood number—should reflect three important tenets to ensure proper motivation for the CEO, appropriate alignment with the interests of shareholders, and understanding by the wider employee population. First, a CEO's overall compensation should be competitive with that of CEOs in other comparable organizations that compete for similar talent. Second, the CEO's compensation (particularly annual and longer-term incentive awards) should vary appropriately with the company's business results. Third, the CEO's compensation should be clearly communicated. Public companies in many countries are required to publicly disclose their CEOs' pay arrangements. In the United States, anyone can find out what the CEO of a publicly traded company makes by reading the company's proxy statement (freely accessible online) filed annually with the Securities and Exchange Commission (SEC). Shareholders and employees at even successfully run companies often question the size of the CEO's paycheck. This challenge can be addressed by clearly communicating the philosophy, mechanics, timing, and rationale for each of the elements of the CEO's pay.

In Closing: The Rewarded Employee

Since 2002, Kevin Carter has been a server at Craftsteak, award-winning chef Tom Colicchio's restaurant at MGM Grand. Each day, Carter serves up Kobe beef and lobster to guests who spend an average $108 per meal.

A forty-eight-year-old husband and father, Carter came to Las Vegas in 1985 after waiting tables in Detroit. He joined MGM Grand in the early 1990s and witnessed the property's transformation under Gamal Aziz. As a star performer, Carter has come to exemplify the consistently high level of guest service that is the cornerstone of Aziz's competitive strategy.

In 2004, Carter was named Employee of the Year, MGM Grand's highest employee honor. Carter talks about what the recognition meant to him:

> It was the best present I ever had, not just because I won, but because of the way they did it . . . and my wife loved it, she was talking about the gala days before it even happened, and she had tears in her eye in the limo, and when they called my name I had my head down and she just screamed and said, "You won you won you won!" They asked me to come to the microphone and talk about how I felt winning, and it just swept me away. I felt like I had arrived because someone recognized what I did every day. I come to work. I care about what I do, and someone actually recognized it.

MGM spends millions on employees here because we are worth it; at least that's what the company tells us. And just because you won one year they do not forget about you. Past winners come back to the gala every year, and they expect you to be a shining example every day. Winning gave me a lot more loyalty, even more than I had.

Below, Carter explains how his engagement translates to MGM Grand's customers and helped Craftsteak earn AAA's coveted Four Diamond Award:

Guests can go to any other venue in this town, and this town is loaded with venues! I can't just go through the motions. My job is to deliver an "experience." No one wants to pay $100 for a steak and have a waiter with a bad attitude . . . every day I come to work and do the right thing, even when people aren't looking I set the example. When fellow employees see you do the right thing, they recognize it. One thing about waiting tables, every day is a new game. I don't care what you did yesterday, what can you do for me today? You have to give the people who saved all their money for an anniversary dinner the same service as you give the guy buying the $5,000 bottle of wine. I'm all about that.

No doubt Carter was engaged before he won, but no tip or wage raise could have rewarded his discretionary efforts—and encouraged them in the future—with the same emotional power as the red-carpet recognition he received. In return, MGM Grand retains an engaged server whose track record for pleasing guests continues.

7

Key Acts of Engagement

How Leaders at All Levels Can Drive Engagement

Engagement is not so much a company
program as a way of life.
—*Michelle Clements, Senior Vice President*
of Human Resources, REI

Employee engagement is an invaluable intangible that can never be bought but can always be earned. It can be elusive for some companies and seemingly unattainable for others. But every company and every leader have the opportunity to earn and nurture employee engagement, and, if successful, to achieve results that dramatically and consistently surpass the results of those companies that ignore it or take it for granted.

Engagement does not spring forth from a single person, action, or policy. Rather, as we've seen throughout the book, there is a broad array of engagement drivers—leadership and management behaviors, company-wide programs, formal procedures, and cultural philosophies—that, if fully utilized, enable company leadership to tap into the considerable and valuable reserves of discretionary effort that employees are quite willing to offer.

Unfortunately, driving engagement remains a challenge for too many organizations. Our *Global Workforce Study* indicates that's because many leaders do not yet truly understand the critical role they play in the engagement equation and have, to a certain extent, lost sight of both their power and their responsibility to drive it. Two myths have led us here. The first myth is that workers themselves are the problem. Many leaders see employees as lazy, cynical, or just out for themselves. Engagement, therefore, becomes a function of the people an organization is lucky enough to find and hire. The second myth, which we looked at earlier, is that engagement comes down to an employee's direct boss, his or her manager. So, assuming an organization has its fair share of the innately engaged people, maintaining that engagement is up to the direct boss.

Neither of these assumptions is accurate. Today's employees want to be challenged, they're willing to work hard, and they're coming to understand that they must take an increasing degree of responsibility for their own employment experience. According to our study, only 11 percent of employees said they do not set high standards for themselves. What's more, 86 percent agreed they set high goals for themselves in terms of their work. Most organizations have a ready, willing, and capable reservoir of talent, energy, and dedication. But it's up to them to tap it in meaningful ways. And, as we have shown, direct bosses are critical catalysts of engagement, but without engaging programs and policies set up by the organization—and engaging behaviors from the most visible senior leaders—direct bosses' efforts will fail to deliver full engagement.

Discretionary effort doesn't just materialize. It's largely up to companies themselves—and their leaders—to elicit that effort. As we noted earlier, our study clearly shows the primacy of the *organization* (versus the individual manager) in creating the conditions that drive engagement, particularly senior leadership's actions and behavior, learning and development opportunities, and the company's image and reputation. These conditions are shaped by the engaging actions of four interdependent groups:

- The CEO and senior leaders.
- Direct bosses, managers, and supervisors.
- Human resources (HR) professionals, as well as other operational groups, such as corporate communications.
- Individual workers.

While there isn't a standard engagement recipe for each of these groups, there are specific actions that could serve as a starting point for senior leaders, HR professionals, and bosses to develop their plans to help Know, Grow, Inspire, Involve, and Reward employees. And there are ways that workers can give back to the organization, and take responsibility for their own work experiences.

Distilled from the real-life activities at the Engaging Eight organizations, as well as our own experience and research, this starting point can help take your organization, your department, and you to the next engagement level. The result, of course, is improved energy and performance—and discretionary effort— among your most valuable workers.

How CEOs and Senior Executives Can Drive Engagement

Senior leaders play a critical role in closing whatever engagement gap exists in your organization, in large part because they hold power over the number one engagement driver in the United States and globally: employees' need to believe their senior leaders truly care about their well-being. Everything the CEO and his or her colleagues do and say—and how they say it—cascades down to affect people's behaviors. Philosophies formed and communicated at the top are the foundation of corporate culture and guide decisions at every level. Senior executives must set an example by leading in an engaging manner and giving employees the tools, resources, and permission to do their best work.

Now, the problem: Only 1 in 10 of the 88,000 respondents in our *Global Workforce Study* agreed that their organization's senior leaders treat employees as vital corporate assets. A larger percentage reported that their leaders act as if employees don't matter. In short, senior leaders may say publicly and proudly that employees are their most important assets, but their actions and interactions with employees are delivering a very different message. And this perception-reality gap represents an opportunity to drive improved performance.

Our interactions with hundreds of CEOs and senior executives, and comments from thousands of people—via research and directly—reveal an unavoidable truth: engagement flows downhill or it doesn't flow at all. If the senior team doesn't truly believe that individuals' decisions to exert or withhold discretionary effort are an important competitive differentiator, then employee engagement will remain elusive. Every action and every word from the top set a precedent for expected and acceptable behavior. C-level executives must treat their executive teams in the same ways they want every manager in the organization to treat their direct reports. While it may not be the easiest of tasks, we have seen numerous examples throughout this book of corporate leaders who have won the hearts and minds of their employees, even from afar. Below are examples from our engaging leaders, along with some ideas we discussed earlier, that ensure that engagement flows from the top and, inevitably, throughout the organization.

Know Them

- Recognize that an organization's culture, processes, and priorities have a greater effect on engagement levels than the behaviors of individual bosses.

- Know the characteristics of your organization's unique workforce, especially its most critical subgroups. Implement a formal method to annually capture employees' attitudes, needs, and work patterns so you understand workers as much as you understand customers.

- Know the executive team. Each member of this group brings personal aspirations to the job, as well as challenges outside of work. Help them meet their goals and they will help the company meet its goals.

- Make an effort to know the workforce via personal touch. Whether you schedule small, casual Q&A sessions with functional and regional work groups, or drop in on employees at work, your effort will be noted. To encourage candid conversations, speak to employees without their supervisor present.

- Respect your role as a direct boss, and get to know the organization's most influential people one-on-one.

Grow Them

- Embrace your own ongoing education and actively share newfound knowledge with people around you. Find new learning opportunities, such as talking to midlevel software developers about the latest technologies or attending international conferences that put you in touch with economic, political, and topical experts.

- Champion ongoing education throughout the organization. Use a grand gesture that speaks to the entire organization by virtue of its breadth and scale to symbolically and practically communicate leadership's dedication to ongoing learning at every level.

- Emphasize growth opportunities for high performers throughout the organization. The most productive, successful, and ambitious workers require constant challenge in their professional lives and have a great appetite for personal growth. Feed that appetite so this critical cohort stays with the company, remains productive, and infuses colleagues with their enthusiasm.

- Hold managers accountable for developing and growing their own direct reports. Accountability breeds action. When bosses are held accountable and judged on the degree to which they help grow their direct reports, these managers are more likely to take an active role in this area.

- Foster a safe environment to fail, especially if innovation is a cornerstone of the company's competitive advantage. Ensure that fear and caution do not replace creativity and risk taking. Leaders' failure to accept imperfection will hinder the intellectual growth that is a key to engagement and organizational growth.

Inspire Them

- Combine operational prowess with the personal touch. People are inspired to perform and deliver for leaders they come to know, trust, and respect. Senior leaders need to be accessible and visible.

- Emphasize that *how* business is conducted is as critical as *what* is achieved. Create and communicate company-wide values that inspire people to do the most appropriate thing even when no one is watching.

- Insist that the organization support local and global philanthropic initiatives that correspond to its mission.
- Empathize with people by finding and sharing common ground. Treat individuals at every level of the organization with respect. It will be noted.

Involve Them

- Communicate to the organization clearly, honestly, and frequently. To be perceived as sincere, acknowledge rather than avoid internal and external challenges, and discuss what the organization is doing to combat them.
- Routinely articulate organizational priorities and values so people are equipped to focus their daily activities in ways that ensure the organization moves in the right direction.
- Give people freedom to reach clearly agreed-upon goals and objectives within a strategic and ethical framework dictated from the highest levels.
- Ask, listen, answer. Solicit questions from individual employees and consider ideas from all levels of the workforce. Actively explain the process and rationale behind major decisions and even those who disagree will appreciate the insight.
- Allow freedom, time, and resources for employees to collect and share information that can improve the way work gets done.

Reward Them

- Tolerate nothing less than fair pay for all, globally. And if you say you pay for performance, make sure that distinct differences in performance levels are accompanied by corresponding distinct differences in rewards.

- Ensure that your organization delivers competitive and fair benefits packages that adequately address employees' diverse needs, while also meeting the organization's cost objectives.
- Dispense recognition and show appreciation, in person and in public.
- Hold senior leader accountable for driving employee engagement by tying a portion of annual bonuses to improvements in engagement scores.

While not all the CEOs with whom we spoke use the term *engagement,* all of them subscribe to engagement's main premise. They believe, wholeheartedly, that if they and the organization give employees more than just money—if they actively try to Know, Grow, Inspire, Involve, and fairly Reward people—then workers will respond by going the extra mile.

How HR Professionals and Other Leaders Can Drive Engagement Throughout the Organization

Creating and administering programs that support all aspects of the employee experience is an essential responsibility of human resources experts and departments. Indeed, a majority of formal programs and procedures that affect engagement levels are driven by HR. These internal professionals must translate senior leaders' philosophies into concrete tactics that help the organization Know, Grow, Involve, Inspire, and Reward the workforce.

While basics such as pay and benefits may not directly drive engagement, they are still important. Get them wrong and people will leave. But getting them right is not enough to yield better engagement. As we have shown throughout the book, workers care deeply about many things other than compensation that HR can help control, such as educational opportunities, wellness policies, and formal recognition. There is no doubt that an organization's HR activities are an integral part of the engagement equation.

Know Them

- Routinely measure the degree to which employees grasp the company's overall direction to ensure that the messages, values, and priorities are sinking in.
- Approach employee research with the same strategic and tactical finesse that the organization approaches consumer research.
- Design annual or biannual employee surveys that guarantee employee confidentiality and are easy to access. Encourage employee participation in surveys by formally promoting their purpose.
- Share workforce survey results—the positive and the negative— with the executive team and with employees. Prioritize company-wide actions that will bridge employee engagement gaps and simultaneously reinforce the organization's strategy and mission.
- Compare internal workforce data to norms derived from competitors, high-performing companies, and the organization's own historic research to better interpret results and prioritize follow-up actions.
- Synthesize information gleaned from personal interactions, employee surveys, and workforce metrics to gain a macrolevel understanding of your employee population.
- Know which employees most directly affect organizational performance and profitability. Segment employee groups into four categories: strategic, core, support, and noncore.
- Focus on select areas that will have the most positive impact,

in part by focusing changes on employees in strategic or core roles.

Grow Them

- Align training opportunities and curricula with business strategy and performance goals. Ensure that training programs reinforce employee behaviors and skills that are required to meet the organization's goals and deliver against its mission.

- Establish a flexible training curriculum that provides opportunities for personalized growth experiences via a mix of learning activities.

- Incorporate a variety of real-world problem-solving activities into the educational and work experience.

- Build talent from within based on competencies that support the company's business goals. At the same time, expose employees to teachers from outside the organization, including customers, academics, authors, and subject matter experts.

- Put teeth into performance management, treating it as a formal process, not simply a technological "fill-in-the-box" requirement once or twice a year. Create review procedures that are easy to follow, and ensure that employees understand opportunities and requirements for career advancement within the organization.

- Use formal courses, mentor relationships, written materials, and sharing of best practices to teach managers how to lead people and consistently improve their management skills.

Inspire Them

- Help the organization cultivate a brag-worthy corporate reputation through external validations. Communicate any external praise and validation that the company receives to the workforce, community, and industry.

- Establish venues to share organizational, team, and employee successes with the entire workforce on a regular basis. Strive for a steady flow of good news—from minor contributions to major achievements—that speaks for itself.
- To foster pride throughout the workforce, articulate connections between an organization's outputs—be it products or charitable deeds—and a greater good.

Involve Them

- Create a business-literate workforce via formal courses and easily accessible materials that explain the organization's business, core processes, and market position, and that provide appropriate, accurate, and current data regarding ongoing operations, products, and services.
- Help managers draw a clear line of sight for their direct reports. Equip every boss with the ability to show employees how their day-to-day responsibilities ultimately contribute to product quality, customer experiences, the corporate brand, and the organization's overall profitability.
- Establish formal feedback instruments—a suggestion box, an idea blog—where employees can easily offer input. Complete the feedback loop so people know their ideas were heard.

Reward Them

- Encourage employees to recognize the contributions of their colleagues and direct reports. Create and distribute recognition tools that people can access quickly and easily. Use similar tools to encourage customers and vendors to thank workers for exceptional service.

- Publicly reward performance and valued behaviors. Establish formal award and recognition programs that reinforce the organization's values at local and global levels.
- Understand what your employee population values most, and design benefits and compensation packages that balance those values with organizational cost considerations.
- Design fair, competitive compensation and career-development programs and opportunities that are clearly communicated to the workforce and fairly executed by managers.

Human resources plays an invaluable role when it comes to executing engaging initiatives. HR professionals structure and oversee the very policies and programs that bring senior leaders' philosophies to life. To paraphrase EMC's head of HR, Jack Mollen: innovation is not just something that applies to a company's products and services, but to the overall business operations. We agree. If ever there was a time in history for innovative people management strategies and practices, this is it.

How Every Boss and Manager Can Engage Direct Reports

Workers' direct bosses have tremendous, though not exclusive, control over how people feel about their jobs every day, and the level at which they perform. Research has consistently found that one of the top reasons people quit is because of their supervisor. And as the primary channel through which corporate philosophies are communicated and programs are accessed, bosses are crucial to engaging individuals.

That said, front-line managers still fall short of their potential to

Know, Grow, Inspire, Involve, and Reward. Our *Global Workforce Study* bears this out:

- Only 43 percent of workers worldwide think their immediate supervisor understands and motivates them.
- The same percentage believe their immediate manager coaches and builds employees' strengths (leaving more than half who do not).
- Only 44 percent agree that their boss inspires enthusiasm for work.
- Just 53 percent say that their supervisor encourages and empowers people to take initiative in their work.
- Only 44 percent say their manager consults employees before making decisions that affect them.
- Just 59 percent of workers worldwide believe their immediate manager recognizes and appreciates good work.

These data represent prominent gaps that can and must be bridged. The following tactics can help managers do just that.

Know Them
- Review and understand your company's overall employee research results.
- Encourage your direct reports' participation in company-wide employee research.
- Share local employee survey results with your direct reports, working with them to identify actions that will bridge local engagement gaps.
- Invest time in conversation. Commit to understanding what motivates individual workers—particularly high performers—in a manner that suits your personality and style.

- Use what you learn about individuals to guide them toward company programs and opportunities, and to inform how you manage them day to day.

Grow Them

- Take time to understand individual learning styles, interests, and career aspirations—and realize that these will change over time for each individual. Help people manage their careers by identifying skills they must develop in the short and long term, and connect them with traditional and nontraditional career paths in the organization.
- Provide direct reports with information about company-sponsored learning opportunities, such as training courses, tuition reimbursement programs, and shadowing. Encourage and accommodate their participation.
- Help direct reports connect with experts and colleagues throughout the organization who can mentor them or add to their own learning experiences.
- Solicit and welcome employee questions regarding the organization's products, services, and procedures. When people feel free to discuss what they do *not* know, they'll plug knowledge holes and go forward with more confidence and the right information.
- Grow your own management skills. Be honest about your own deficits as a leader, and make an effort to improve via formal training, reading, and consulting with leaders you respect.

Inspire Them

- Manage with empathy, honesty, and visibility while maintaining high performance standards.

- Role-model acceptable and ethical behavior in every interaction.
- Meet with direct reports one-on-one. Listen, refrain from judgment, and integrate what you learn about them into your work relationship.
- Strive to be a best boss, not a best friend. Inform employees about why and how decisions were made.
- Be visible and accessible in good times and bad. When walking the halls or the factory floor, remember that every act reverberates with and is interpreted by employees.
- Listen to employees' concerns, prioritize them, and act to remedy problems when productive and appropriate.

Involve Them

- Dispense daily data and any relevant information—the status of ongoing projects, nearing deadlines, customer issues—that will better inform people's activities and decisions.
- Be a pipeline for the company's big picture. Keep everyone in the department informed about changes in operations and the marketplace, and make sure they have a line of sight between their work and the company's strategic objectives.
- Invite input and listen with an open mind. Ask direct reports how you, as well as the organization, can improve, and let people know their opinions are heard even if their ideas or opinions are not implemented.
- Empower workers to make decisions and act in the best interests of the company and its customers without constant management oversight. Simultaneously, hold people accountable for their actions and responsible for meeting agreed-upon goals.

Reward Them

- Regularly—but as deserved—show direct reports sincere, knowledgeable appreciation and give them fact-based feedback by recognizing something specific they did to help the business or the group.
- Reward people with tangible tokens of appreciation that reflect their personal preferences.
- Be conversant with and able to discuss the organization's compensation and performance review procedures with direct reports knowledgeably and thoroughly. Review employees' performance in accordance with organizational procedures, and follow the rules for everyone, no exceptions.
- Set clear goals so employees know what's expected of them.

While front-line supervisors may not be the primary driver of engagement, they do matter in that they are the most direct connection between an employee and the organization's policies, expectations, and goals. Bottom line for bosses: be honest with the people who work for you. They'll appreciate sincerity more than anything, and respond in turn.

How Individual Employees Can Increase Their Own and Their Colleagues' Engagement

As we've observed throughout this book, engagement is a two-way street, not the sole responsibility of the employer. Employees need to help their managers and organization know their individual preferences, seek growth opportunities, and collaborate with colleagues. It's incumbent on individual employees to take advantage of the range of opportunities their organization offers to create higher levels of engagement.

Our data debunk several stereotypes about the nature of today's workforce: that workers are cubicle clock-watchers who do the minimum to get by, or, conversely, that employees are ambitious free agents loyal only to themselves and their careers. Both our data and our experience tell us employees want to be challenged, to learn and grow, and to have stability and security. We've heard from dozens of engaged employees throughout the book, most of whom played a part in their own level of engagement. The following are a few actions that could play a role for you:

Know Yourself and Others

- Know what drives you to perform, and share that information with your direct supervisor as well as colleagues, even if it means initiating the discussion.
- Help your supervisor use what she knows about you by suggesting ways to help you feel more engaged. Whatever creative ideas you propose (a flexible schedule, for instance), never sacrifice the quality of your work.
- Participate in company-wide employee surveys and provide honest feedback.
- Make an effort to understand what drives your coworkers, so when working together or collaborating in teams, you can more effectively communicate, prioritize, and organize assignments. And make an effort to understand what drives your boss and the types of pressures he or she is also feeling.

Grow Yourself and Others

- Raise your hand. Actively seek out assignments, new roles, or mentors rather than waiting for learning opportunities or people to find you.

- Embrace challenge. Life is boring when we know all the answers. Solving unanticipated problems—even making mistakes—are opportunities to grow. Look for a lesson in every misstep, and take ownership of your actions.

- Take advantage of company-sponsored learning opportunities, and don't hesitate to invent your own career path.

- Insist that your boss tell you where you must improve and what you need to do to get to wherever it is you want to go. Also, ask your manager to identify your strengths and areas where you might help mentor others.

- Most important, know your strengths and weaknesses, and take control of your professional destiny.

Inspire Yourself and Others

- Inspire optimal performance in others by treating peers with empathy, maintaining high expectations of others and yourself, and assisting people as needed.

- Participate in company-sponsored charity or socially responsible initiatives. Encourage colleagues' involvement, and initiate activities that allow the organization to contribute to the community, both globally and locally.

- Share your motivators, career aspirations, and relevant but appropriate details of your life outside work with colleagues and your boss. Coworkers and managers who know what inspires you are more likely to bring such circumstances about.

- Inspire laterally by making colleagues feel valued and valuable. Inspiration is contagious; when you feel inspired, share the feeling and reason with others.

Involve Yourself and Others

- Be an informed participant. Familiarize yourself with the company's status in the marketplace and community. Stay abreast of national and local news stories, read internal newsletters; familiarize yourself with industry bloggers and pundits; and review industry publications and websites.

- Think big picture. Understand how the decisions you make and the work you do contribute to the goals of the organization. If you don't know, ask.

- Be a proactive, compatible collaborator. Get to know people throughout the organization in all departments, and seek them out—with a question or a long-term project—when you need their expertise to reach individual, departmental, and organizational goals. Just as important, assist colleagues when they contact you.

- Look for ways to improve. Think about and share ways that you, your department, and the company can more productively reach goals, deliver products, and serve customers.

- Provide constructive feedback—in person or through company-provided channels—directly to managers and senior executives.

Reward Yourself and Others

- When you reach a milestone or achieve a critical success, acknowledge it and treat yourself. It's important to celebrate and reward our own successes, rather than just waiting for others to do so.

- Recognize colleagues for work well done. When appropriate and legitimate, tell your boss and company leaders what they are doing well. Concrete, specific feedback ("Your presentation clarified an issue for me" versus the more generic "great speech") will prevent productive praise from feeling insincere.

- Take time to understand all the health and financial benefits your employer has made available to you. You cannot take advantage of what you don't know exists.

- Be clear on the organization's pay policies. Understand exactly what's expected of your performance and how it will reflect in your compensation.

- Assess your performance against goals on a quarterly basis to ensure you are on track.

- Know yourself. Be honest about what's most important to you—financially and otherwise—and be willing to sacrifice less valuable monetary rewards for ones that enhance your life. Take stock of the various rewards you receive from your employer in addition to pay—such as recognition, training, flextime—and consider their individual value to you, your future, and your family. Before jumping ship to another organization simply for a pay increase, make sure to evaluate the full portfolio of rewards.

We end on a practical, personal note to help you become a more engaging leader. While we have emphasized that an organization's culture, processes, and priorities have a greater effect on engagement levels than the behaviors of individual bosses, your daily behaviors are nonetheless tremendously important to the engagement equation. Personalizing these five actions—Know, Grow, Inspire, Involve, and Reward—to fit your organization and team is sure to help you engage your workforce and deliver outstanding performance.

The 5 Keys to Engagement

Know Them

Know what's most important to people.

Grow Them

Help them develop new skills and advance their careers.

Inspire Them

Embody your organization's values, and show concern about employees' well-being.

Involve Them

Inform employees how they contribute to the organization's performance, and involve them in business processes.

Reward Them

Appreciate their efforts, and reward them for work well done.

Engagement is the fuel that will drive your people and your organization to succeed as the world of business becomes increasingly complex and competitive. Every organization, every manager, has it within their power to Know, Grow, Inspire, Involve, and Reward their people. When you unlock human potential, you maximize business performance. That's the benefit of closing the engagement gap.

ACKNOWLEDGMENTS

Like many of life's most rewarding and challenging endeavors, this book owes so much to the invaluable support and insight of our teammates and colleagues at Towers Perrin: Gary Berger, Max Caldwell, Miriam Connaughton, Tom Davenport, Roselyn Feinsod, Andy Glover, Ted Jarvis, Ravin Jesuthasan, Patrick Kulesa, Todd Lippincott, Julie Naismith, Judy Nygard, Sandra O'Neal, Emmett Seaborn, Stacey Thaler, and Charlie Watts, as well as Lillian Martin, Angela Velardo, and Nancy Vildoza. A very special thank-you to Sharon Wunderlich who has, for years, unselfishly and patiently helped us develop and translate our ideas and concepts into words, and helped us, and many others at Towers Perrin, determine how best to convey our ideas to broad audiences.

We also wish to thank the employees at every organization we included in the book for candidly sharing their work experiences with us. Specifically, we'd like to acknowledge the efforts of the following people with whom we worked over the course of many months and who helped make their companies' participation possible: Nancy Reardon and Anthony Sanzio from Campbell Soup Company; Polly Pearson at EMC Corporation; Tom Buckmaster, Julie Tenney, and Michael Bennett from Honeywell International; Duke Holliday with McKesson Corp.; Corrine Clement and Miriam Hammond at MGM Grand; Michael Dowling, Dr. Kathleen Gallo, and Marisol Fernandez at North Shore–Long Island Jewish Health System; Elizabeth Flynn from Novartis; and, Michelle Clements and Sandy Willcut from REI.

Don wishes to thank his family. Thanks to my mother, Betty Lee, my brother Bruce, my sons Dustin and Devon, and especially my father, Pete, for their guidance and unwavering support through the years. I also owe a huge debt of gratitude to Towers Perrin and my extended family of clients and coworkers who have driven my personal levels of engagement for twenty-six years.

Julie wishes to thank her husband, Davin, and her sons Dane and Jeffrey, who inspire her and support her in all her endeavors; her parents and siblings, Joe, Anita, Judy, Jeff, Jay, Jeanne, Janine, and Jon Jarecke, for giving her a strong foundation and a hearty work ethic. She is grateful to her fellow "wordies" at Towers Perrin who have encouraged her to focus on stories and words as much as on numbers in her work, and all of her Towers Perrin colleagues who have enabled her to say every year for twenty-one years, "I really love my job."

We also wish to acknowledge our editors at Portfolio, Adrienne Schultz and Adrian Zackheim, and our literary agent, Stuart Krichevsky. Their curiosity and passion for business and people's stories have been helpful in bringing this book to fruition.

And finally, we want to thank Joanne Gordon for collaborating with us to produce our first book. We both love to write and share our ideas, but Joanne is an experienced author without whom we would not have been able to complete this book. Joanne kept us focused on deadlines and on the key messages we wanted to convey while helping us eliminate (most of) our consulting language. She combed through thousands of pages of background materials and interview notes and helped us crystallize our thoughts and convey them succinctly. We are grateful for her partnership and have enjoyed sharing the experience with her. Joanne never showed any signs of an "engagement gap" herself, and we sincerely appreciate her energy, enthusiasm, and commitment.

INDEX